Cambridge Elements

Elements in Beckett Studies
edited by
Dirk Van Hulle
University of Oxford
Mark Nixon
University of Reading

BECKETT AND LEOPARDI

Peter Boxall
University of Oxford
Peter Nicholls
New York University

Shaftesbury Road, Cambridge CB2 8EA, United Kingdom

One Liberty Plaza, 20th Floor, New York, NY 10006, USA

477 Williamstown Road, Port Melbourne, VIC 3207, Australia

314–321, 3rd Floor, Plot 3, Splendor Forum, Jasola District Centre, New Delhi – 110025, India

103 Penang Road, #05–06/07, Visioncrest Commercial, Singapore 238467

Cambridge University Press is part of Cambridge University Press & Assessment, a department of the University of Cambridge.

We share the University's mission to contribute to society through the pursuit of education, learning and research at the highest international levels of excellence.

www.cambridge.org
Information on this title: www.cambridge.org/9781009547918

DOI: 10.1017/9781009431019

© Peter Boxall and Peter Nicholls 2025

This publication is in copyright. Subject to statutory exception and to the provisions of relevant collective licensing agreements, no reproduction of any part may take place without the written permission of Cambridge University Press & Assessment.

When citing this work, please include a reference to the DOI 10.1017/9781009431019

First published 2025

A catalogue record for this publication is available from the British Library

ISBN 978-1-009-54791-8 Hardback
ISBN 978-1-009-43100-2 Paperback
ISSN 2632-0746 (online)
ISSN 2632-0738 (print)

Cambridge University Press & Assessment has no responsibility for the persistence or accuracy of URLs for external or third-party internet websites referred to in this publication and does not guarantee that any content on such websites is, or will remain, accurate or appropriate.

For EU product safety concerns, contact us at Calle de José Abascal, 56, 1°, 28003 Madrid, Spain, or email eugpsr@cambridge.org

Beckett and Leopardi

Elements in Beckett Studies

DOI: 10.1017/9781009431019
First published online: November 2025

Peter Boxall
University of Oxford

Peter Nicholls
New York University

Author for correspondence: Peter Boxall, peter.boxall@ell.ox.ac.uk

Abstract: This Element revisits the relation between Giacomo Leopardi and Samuel Beckett to argue that the dialogue between them might offer new ways of thinking about the nature of both writers' pessimism. The authors suggest that Leopardi becomes increasingly important for Beckett, not only because he frames a literary philosophy of scepticism but because he gives a rich account of the means by which thoroughgoing pessimism might open on to an unenchanted mode of persistence. In doing so, the Element looks past the impasse – between going on and not going on – that threatens to forestall imaginative possibilities for both writers.

Keywords: Giacomo Leopardi, Samuel Beckett, pessimism, persistence, nakedness

© Peter Boxall and Peter Nicholls 2025
ISBNs: 9781009547918 (HB), 9781009431002 (PB), 9781009431019 (OC)
ISSNs: 2632-0746 (online), 2632-0738 (print)

Contents

	Introduction: Affinities	1
	Part I Leopardi/Beckett	7
1	Leopardi's Sceptical Poetics	7
2	The Beating Heart: 'To Himself'	15
3	Voices of the Dead: Leopardi's 'Chorus'	23
	Part II Beckett/Leopardi	33
4	That Narrow Region: *First Love*	33
5	A Spectacle of Nothingness: Beckett's Trilogy	40
6	The World Is Mud: *How It Is*	48
	Conclusion: 'Another Heavenly Day'	59
	References	65

Introduction: Affinities

We began writing this Element not primarily to develop our own research enthusiasms – Beckett, for Boxall, Leopardi, for Nicholls – but rather because we were fascinated by the idea of a 'conversation' between two writers who seemed to have so much in common in terms of character and outlook. Beckett recalled that 'Leopardi was a strong influence when I was young (his pessimism, not his patriotism!)' (2014b, 136), and his humorous dissociation here shows how cleanly he could separate the aristocratic nineteenth-century poet, with his flamboyant nationalism and his fondness for archaic mannerism, from the mordant pessimist in whom Beckett quickly recognised an avatar of the 'modern' spirit. This Element, then, will have less to say about the question of influence as such – Beckett scholars have readily acknowledged that – than about the deep-seated affinities and shared preoccupations that might seem to place these unique bodies of work in a sort of reciprocal relation that is at once intellectual and affective. The writings of Leopardi (1798–1837) and Beckett (1906–89) seem to us increasingly to illuminate each other even as they also harbour similar opacities and areas of unresolved contradiction and impasse. To this end, we have divided this Element into two parts: in the first, we read Leopardi, while looking forward to Beckett; in the second, we read Beckett, while looking back to Leopardi.

On one level, of course, Beckett's regard for Leopardi might be explained straightforwardly by the temperamental and philosophical pessimism the two men seem to have shared, though Daniela Caselli (1996, 2012) has helpfully questioned the simplicity of this assumption. Her conclusion is one from which the present Element takes its initial premise: both writers, she suggests, 'refuse the totalizing power of an absolute negation, and for this neither of them can be labelled nihilistic, and even less pessimistic' (Caselli, 1996, 4). Roberta Cauchi-Santoro (2016) begins her book-length study of the relationship with the same assumption, though, as the following pages will show, we are less persuaded than she that Leopardi and Beckett are primarily concerned with the need for compassion and recognition of the other.[1]

Beckett read Leopardi during his student years at Trinity College, Dublin (1923–7), and there are allusions to the *Canti* throughout his early works.[2] In his first published essay, 'Dante ... Bruno . Vico . . Joyce', Beckett (1972, 17)

---

[1] Cauchi-Santoro's approach differs from ours in her determination to read both writers through an amalgamation of Lacanian and Levinasian theory. On Beckett and Leopardi, see also Cortellessa (2006, 111–20), Bouchard (1999, 77–89) and Furlani (2024, 31–53).

[2] Unless otherwise indicated, the Italian edition of the poems used throughout is Leopardi (1987) and all English translations are by Henry Weinfield who has generously permitted us to use them here. All other translations when not attributed are by Peter Nicholls.

quotes from Leopardi's 'Sopra il monumento di Dante che si perparava in Firenze' ('On the Monument to Dante Being Erected in Florence', 1818) to celebrate Joyce ('il meonio cantor non è più solo', 'Homer doesn't stand alone'), and in a passage in *Dream of Fair to Middling Women* (Beckett, 1992a, 18) he plays on a phrase from Leopardi's 'Le ricordanze' ('The Recollections', 1829).[3] Mark Nixon (2011, 200 n.36) observes that 'The *Watt* notebooks contain a further reference to the "unhappy writer" Leopardi and his poem "Night Song of a Wandering Asiatic Shepherd" (notebook 1, 31 r)'.[4] and it has been suggested that the closing stages of *Endgame* echo the ending of the 'Canto del gallo silvestre' ('Song of the Great Wild Rooster') in Leopardi's *Operette morali* (Barnes, 1989, 45–6). Ruby Cohn (2005, 109) also notes that the protagonist of the Ur-*Watt*, James Quin, is an avid reader of the Italian poet, and Ackerley (2010, 211–12) reads the mention of 'a thicket flower unrecorded' in the 'Addenda' to *Watt* as an allusion to Leopardi's 'Broom' and Mr Hackett's 'hunch' as a nod to the deformity caused by the poet's excessive study in his youth.

Beckett's direct allusions to Leopardi are well-known to critics, then, but there are other cases where the connection is less clear-cut. It is tempting, for example, to wonder if Beckett knew the autobiographical fragment 'Appunti e ricordi' ('Notes and Memories') that Leopardi rapidly drafted in 1819.[5] This erratically punctuated, elliptical fragment with its slippages between first and third person pronouns might recall a similar oscillation in Beckett's *The Unnamable* (in, e.g., Beckett, 1994, 396–7), and several figures and phrases in Leopardi's text seem almost to foreshadow ones developed by Beckett. The comparison of the window of the ark from which Noah launched the dove with 'that window over the stairs' in the Palazzo Leopardi (Leopardi, 1988, 1193) might, for instance, have provided one prompt for the *mise-en-scène* of *Endgame*, a possibility which seems more compelling when we know that the first draft of *Fin de partie* made more extended reference to the story of the Flood (Knowlson, 1996, 336–7). Echoes of this kind are certainly suggestive but, as Caselli (2012, 136) has noted, the absence of any notebooks from the period 1928–30 means that we know little about the texts from which Beckett

---

[3] Leopardi's 'alla fioca lucerne poetando' ('writing poetry by my faint lantern') there becomes 'alla fioca lucerne leggendo Meredith'.

[4] Ackerley (2010) suggests several possible allusions in *Watt* to Leopardi's 'Canto notturno': 212.2 ('a fascio of white light'), 217.1 ('an encountered nightsong'), 222.6 ('universal splendour') and 225.4 ('night wanderer'). He also finds in the typescript of the novel possible allusions to 'La ginestra' ('Broom') (Ackerley, 2010, 211, 214). Byron (2022) considers the more extensive allusions to 'Canto notturno' in the manuscript of *Watt* and Beckett's way of connecting them with Wordsworth's 'Salisbury Plain'.

[5] The fragment was first published in Leopardi (1906). After D'Intino (1995), the text has been referred to as *Vita abbozzata di Silvio Sarno*.

drew his first knowledge of the poet. A recent catalogue of his library as it remained at his death does, however, give us a little more information, showing that at some point (and obviously after the composition of his Proust essay) he acquired a 1936 edition of *I Canti* (edited by Ettore Fabietti) along with a copy of Leopardi's *Prose, con uno studio di Pietro Giordani*, undated but a reprint of the 1913 first edition of the same text (Van Hulle and Nixon, 2013, 276). Beckett's copies of these works are not annotated, as Caselli (2012, 146 n.8) ascertained, but they do tell us several things that may add significantly to the allusions we have already noted. First, the *Prose* contains the *Operette morali* which may well have provided Beckett with an introduction to Leopardi's satirical mode and to the pessimistic materialism that predicted the sentiments of the poem that was to remain of central importance to Beckett, 'A se stesso' ('To Himself'). The *Prose* also includes the *Pensieri*, the acerbic thoughts and maxims that at the end of his life Leopardi culled for publication from his voluminous private journal, the *Zibaldone*.[6] Perhaps most importantly, though, Fabietti's *Canti* prints as a free-standing poem the 'Coro di morti' ('Chorus of the Dead'), which provided the epigraph to the 'Dialogue between Frederick Ruysch and His Mummies'; most subsequent editors would present the poem only as the epigraph to the 'Dialogue'. We shall suggest in Section 3 that the 'Chorus' might have contributed significantly to Beckett's thoughts on death and dying.

With these two editions of Leopardi's works in hand, it is tempting to assume that Beckett's knowledge of the Italian poet may have extended well beyond the texts indicated by his occasional allusions. Indeed, we shall propose in Section 2 that the more systematic use he made of Leopardi's 'To Himself' reveals the longer reach of the Italian poet's influence. For it was in this poem that Beckett seems to have discovered a certain kind of 'nakedness' – stylistic and experiential – that would define an outer limit of all his work to come. He quotes from 'To Himself' in his first novel, *Dream of Fair to Middling Women*: 'All day he told the beads of his spleen. *Or posa per sempre* [Now you may rest forever] for example he was liable to murmur, lifting and shifting the seat of the disturbance, *stanco mio cor. Assai palpitasti* [worn-out heart. You've beaten long enough] ... and as much more of that gloomy composition as he could remember' (Beckett, 1992a, 62). The poem is humorously recalled in the later *Molloy* (Beckett, 1994, 35–6), and phrases from it figure several times in Beckett's letters. Most frequently, the reference is to the lines 'Non che la speme, il desiderio è spento' ('Not only hope but even the desire / For sweet illusions is now spent in us'). Beckett invokes Leopardi's bleak statement at

---

[6] The edition of the *Zibaldone* used throughout is Leopardi (2013a) and abbreviated reference is made to Z and, following usual practice, Leopardi's manuscript page number (e.g., Z1234).

times of his own self-doubt – 'I feel I am further than ever from being able to write' (2009, 509) – or when 'the same old stupefying routine' makes work 'unthinkable' (2016, 624). In another letter, Beckett recalls that a key phrase from 'To Himself', 'e fango è il mondo', and the world is mud, served as an epigraph for his 1931 essay on Proust (2014b, 136).

That world which Leopardi also described in his *Operette morali* as 'a handful of mud' ('un pugno di fango'; Leopardi, 1982, 417–19) would arguably provide one instigation for the setting of Beckett's *How It Is* (1961), as we suggest in Section 6, and also perhaps find an echo in his description of the world as a 'muckball' in *Krapp's Last Tape* (Beckett, 2006, 222) and *Dream*'s 'Cartesian earthball' (1992a, 134). Used as the epigraph to his essay on Proust, and unaccountably withdrawn when it was republished in 1965, the phrase proleptically associates the Italian poet with Schopenhauer and Proust. As Beckett remarked in an early letter of 1930 to Thomas MacGreevy, 'I am reading Schopenhauer. [. . .] An intellectual justification of unhappiness – the greatest that has ever been attempted – is worth the examination of one who is interested in Leopardi & Proust rather than in Carducci & Barrès' (2009, 33). Leopardi is quoted several times in the essay, with the line from 'To Himself' about the extinction of hope and desire exemplifying, Beckett says, 'the wisdom of all the sages, from Brahma to Leopardi, the wisdom that consists not in the satisfaction but in the ablation of desire' (1965, 18). Later in the essay, Beckett quotes part of those lines again to characterise the wisdom that 'consists in obliterating the faculty of suffering rather than in a vain attempt to reduce the stimuli that exasperate that faculty' (63). 'Ablation': excision, removal, erosion – this grimly surgical word emphasises the deliberateness of an intellectual operation by which the objects of human hopes, beliefs, and desires might be 'obliterated', so leaving the subject painfully exposed but at the same time liberated from illusions of truth and satisfaction. Beckett's early fascination with Leopardi's 'justification of unhappiness' is inflected, of course, by his own temperamental pessimism but, as we shall see in the next section, it is the sceptical temper of the Italian poet's thought that suggests the imaginative conditions of Beckett's art. The distinction here goes deep in each writer's work, a distinction between, on the one hand, a recurring emotional state that accepts a limited horizon in advance and, on the other, a habit of intellectual inquiry that, as Leopardi puts it, 'essentially consists in doubt, and whoever doubts knows, and knows as much as one can know' (Z1655).

While the pessimistic posture acknowledges its own disability and passivity but assigns blame for these elsewhere, scepticism promises a kind of imaginative power, a dynamism defined above all, as we shall see, by its curious persistence. We could put this distinction another way, as poet Yves Bonnefoy does in his study of Leopardi: while pessimism is reducible to a discourse of generalities about humanity's unhappy condition, its separation from nature and so forth, a deliberately doubtful thinking may transport us into the 'unending spaces' of Leopardi's 'L'infinito' where ambiguity and uncertainty perform a ritual hesitation 'between the words of desiring imagination and those of conceptual thought' (Bonnefoy, 2001, 17; 2012, ix). Bonnefoy here supplies a succinct statement of his own poetic aims, but he also contributes to a debate about Leopardi that the philosopher Benedetto Croce had initiated back in 1923. Croce admired Leopardi as a great lyric poet but he cautioned against regarding him as a philosopher of any significance. Pessimism does not amount to an authentic philosophical stance, in his view: 'Philosophy, in so far as it is pessimistic or optimistic, is always in itself pseudo-philosophy [...]. Frank and serious philosophy neither weeps nor laughs but pauses to investigate the forms of being, the working of spirit' (Croce, 1923, 105). When Croce thinks of 'philosophy', of course, he thinks of the pursuit of truth and essence; Leopardi's focus is significantly different, and his conception of what he calls on one occasion 'ultra-philosophy' is based on 'neither philosophy nor reason [... but on] virtue, illusions and enthusiasm'; it is not an attempt to grasp God or the Hegelian Idea but rather a thinking that 'brings us close again to nature' ('ci ravvicini alla natura'; Z115). But, for Croce, when Leopardi is not writing pure, 'idyllic' poetry, he is producing 'non-poetry', with lyric ambition undermined by 'oratory, an indictment, a series of questions', and poetic style becoming 'dry and compressed' and, finally, 'rhetorical' rather than poetic or dramatic (Croce, 1923, 114, 117). Bonnefoy does acknowledge a 'discursive' tendency in Leopardi that risks the reduction of lived experience to the generalities of pessimism (Bonnefoy, 2001, 18), but he observes there a compensatory evocation of a non-conceptual 'presence' that derives from the musicality of the verse. For Bonnefoy, Leopardi is the first definitively modern poet because he is 'the first truly lucid poet' (15), meaning by this that he was the first whose atheism freed him from the lingering transcendental hopes indulged by other writers of the period. At the same time, though, lucidity of vision is not in itself enough: Leopardi, says Bonnefoy, knew that concepts have a material foundation in sound, and so he 'interiorised this music in his poems, allowing them to detach themselves from the negative vision which a too intellectual lucidity encourages, and to produce another kind of vision of beauty and the good' (25). That music is, too, the vehicle of memory, and Bonnefoy reminds us that the Italian word 'ricordanza' ('remembrance') contains within it the word for 'heart' ['cor'] that, for both Leopardi and Beckett, would express the unresolvable contradiction between the indefatigable demands of 'existence', on the one hand, and the always elusive release from them, on the other.

The limits of interpretation, in both writers, have been marked by this unresolvability. In finding itself stranded between the demand to be and the demand not to be, the demand to continue and the demand to cease, the critical faculty exhausts itself. Such blank aporias lead to the famous dead end at the close of *The Unnamable* ('I can't go on, I'll go on'; Beckett, 1994, 418) and to its excruciating extension in *Texts for Nothing*, where the narrative voice acknowledges that 'it can't speak, it can't cease': 'And were the voice quite to cease at last, the old ceasing voice, it would not be true, as it is not true that it speaks' (1995, 154). In what follows, we do not claim to have overcome this contradiction, or to have resolved the chiastic antinomy that shapes the attitude of both writers to hope and to despair (in which, as in *Waiting for Godot*, salvation and damnation cancel each other out; 2006, 14). But in imagining a dialogue between Beckett and Leopardi, we suggest that one can approach a 'region', to use a word important to Beckett, located within the poles of that contradiction.

This is a region that we can find in the work of both writers – it is also a region that stretches between them, and that it is our aim here to map. In Part I, we lay out the forms in which Leopardi's species of poetic pessimism lays the ground for Beckett's. Section 1 characterises what we call here Leopardi's 'sceptical poetics', giving an account of the way that his poetry fashions a particular 'ground', a form of materialist politics that emerges from his sceptical disavowal of the political. Section 2 focuses on the poem 'To Himself', to which Beckett most insistently returns. This poem, in addressing the beating heart as a kind of mechanical object, lays out the forms of self-estrangement that power both Leopardi's and Beckett's poetics. Section 3 then focuses on the posthumous voice, fashioned in Leopardi's 'Chorus of the Dead', a voice which echoes throughout Beckett's work, from *Dream* to *Ghost Trio*. In Part II, we reverse the direction of our reading, looking back from Beckett to Leopardi. In Section 4, we find the region shared by Leopardi and Beckett as it is manifest in Beckett's early novella *First Love*, which we see as a reworking of Leopardi's two texts 'Il primo amore' ('First Love') and *Memorie del primo amore* (*Memories of First Love*). In Section 5, we explore this region, composed at once of life and death, of something and nothing, as it develops in Beckett's prose, from *Watt* to *The Unnamable*. And finally, in Section 6, we find this region given its fullest articulation in Beckett's most difficult and excruciating work *How It Is*. The mud of this text, we argue, is drawn in part from the line in 'To Himself' that Beckett admired, 'e fango è il mondo', 'The world is mud'. It is a kind of *stuff* that Beckett and Leopardi between them fashion, and that is the very ground of their imagination.

Part I Leopardi/Beckett

1 Leopardi's Sceptical Poetics

One way of approaching Leopardi's scepticism is by gauging its effect on his later admirer Friedrich Nietzsche. In a well-known passage in his *Will to Power*, for example, Nietzsche (1968, 221) complains of philosophers that 'they have trusted in concepts as completely as they have mistrusted the senses: they have not stopped to consider that concepts and words are our inheritance from ages in which thinking was very modest and unclear'. 'What is needed above all', Nietzsche continues, 'is an absolute scepticism toward all inherited concepts' (221). This scepticism is necessary not just because concepts become outworn and unreliable, compelling us to create new ones, but also because philosophers, in cleaving to their concepts, have shown themselves to be 'prejudiced against appearance, change, pain, death, the corporeal, the senses, fate and bondage, the aimless' (220). Nietzsche's list of excluded themes that a properly sceptical attitude should re-engage also provides, of course, a rich catalogue of poetry's traditional topoi. Indeed, Nietzsche's list also evokes the major interconnected themes of Leopardi, the writer he called 'perhaps the greatest stylist of the century' (qtd in Murphy, 2012, 136), and whose very name was already a byword for a radical scepticism.

Leopardi may not figure prominently as an originator of modern poetry on our current cultural maps where he is almost wholly, and perhaps unfairly, eclipsed by Baudelaire, but it is nonetheless worth asking what the story of modernism's emergence might look like if we took the hint from Beckett's epigraph to his essay on Proust and located its inaugural moment in Leopardi's poetry rather than in Baudelaire's. It would begin not with a sense of innovation – with Walter Benjamin's emphasis on the *first* appearance of gas lighting, the *first* use of iron as a building material and so on (Singh, 2012, 415 n.8) – but rather with a chilling sense of modernity as something already ruined by the failure of Enlightenment values and the French Revolution (Sanguinetti, 2000). Like Baudelaire, Leopardi pours scorn on the new religion of 'progress', but unlike Baudelaire he finds no promise of intoxication in modernity, which he dismisses in his poem 'Ad Angelo Mai' ('To Angelo Mai', 1820) as a 'dead century' (Leopardi, 1987, 16) in which nature stands starkly revealed both as indifferent to humanity and as a source of its constant suffering. The life of modern man is, for Leopardi, perpetually shadowed by death, an affliction memorably described in his *Zibaldone*: 'I am, pardon the metaphor, a walking sepulchre, and inside me I carry a dead man, a once very sensitive heart that feels no more, etc.' (Z4149).

Leopardi's negativity does not, however, fully explain the nature of his reception in the twentieth century and beyond. Indeed, in Italy his writings have proved a generative source for new formulations of the political. Works by prominent figures on the Left such as Antonio Negri, Roberto Esposito and Massimo Cacciari represent what Esposito calls a 'non-philosophical' strand in Italian thinking that runs counter to the mainstream of European philosophy with its gestures of abstraction and exclusion, and attends instead to what Esposito calls 'life, in its material grain' (2012, 108). Leopardi's materialism has proved an important point of reference for this kind of 'realism' or 'immanentism', inviting some interesting questions about the relation of poetry and poetics to this new political thinking. To the Anglo-American eye, this praise of Leopardi by some of Italy's best-known public intellectuals is perhaps a little unexpected. Leopardi may be, with Petrarch and Dante, one of the country's three foundational poets, but he has been consistently caricatured by non-Italians as a melancholy romantic marooned in the stagnating papal state of the Marche and far removed from all those exciting provocations of *modernité* to which Baudelaire was so subtly and ambivalently attuned. When the young Beckett spoke of 'To Himself' as a 'gloomy composition', he was doing little more than echoing a cliché that came as easily to T. S. Eliot as it had done to the Victorians.[7] The latter, of course, had acknowledged Leopardi as a sublimely lyrical poet, but they also tended to see him as a damagingly pessimistic one; when his philosophical scepticism was acknowledged, by William Gladstone and other early readers, it was generally with regret for the dangerous atheism that accompanied it (see Singh, 1968). Swinburne's regard for him as a powerful civic poet was an honourable exception, though advocacy from Swinburne would not help Leopardi's reputation much in the longer term. It would take critics of a more analytic temper to look beyond the limiting view of Leopardi as merely a pessimist – Walter Benjamin, for example, who wrote in 1928 that 'In this poet, the contemplative and resigned type of the pessimist is contrasted by a different one – that of the paradoxical pragmatist, the ironic angel' (qtd in Rennie, 2005, 140 n.46). As a critic of modernity, Leopardi was by this time coming to seem the very type of the alienated modern; as Antonio Gramsci observed,

> In Leopardi we find, in extremely dramatic form, the crisis of transition to modern man; the critical abandonment of all transcendental conceptions without having found a new moral and intellectual *ubi consistam*, which imparts the same certainty that has been forsaken. (1994, 206–7)

---

[7] See Eliot (2019, 688) where he describes Leopardi as 'a gloomy cuss' in a letter to Ezra Pound.

Gramsci discerns in Leopardi's 'doubtful thinking' a vital if uneasy legacy to 'modern man': for the poet bequeaths a scepticism uncompromised by the fideism that so often shadows weaker versions of the posture, and one that in its radical act of materialist 'abandonment', as Gramsci calls it, leaves the poet defiantly without 'an *ubi consistam*', a place or ground on which to stand.

Gramsci, of course, found his own source of certainty in Marxism, but his recognition of Leopardi's negativity as something more than temperamental melancholy would be increasingly important to later readings of the poet's work. From the 1940s on, accounts like Cesare Luporini's *Leopardi progressivo* (1947) and early essays by Franco Fortini (1946) questioned the traditional romantic construal of Leopardi, leading to a series of politically inflected studies by scholars such as Walter Binni, Antonio Negri, Fabio Russo, Antonio Prete and others. Sebastiano Timpanaro, for example, in the first serious discussion of this question in English, discerned in Leopardi's 'pessimistic materialism' a kind of non-dialectical resource for Marxism, one that, for the poet himself, however, as he adopted a more consistently materialist position, 'acted as a disincentive, at least initially, to any political engagement' (Timpanaro, 1979, 40). In making that dissociation, Timpanaro's contribution to 'the battle for Leopardi', as he called it (34), resonated with earlier left-wing readings such as Fortini's (1946) more pragmatically Marxist repudiation of politically blinkered appropriations of Leopardi for the 'sentimental sublime' and Binni's (1947), with its emphasis on the 'anti-idyllic' aspect of the poet's work. Importantly, Timpanaro also criticised Luporini's suggestion that Leopardi had 'reached the very threshold of dialectical thought', noting that such a proposal 'involves a failure to recognize the wholly practical, sensist-hedonist character of Leopardian pessimism' (1979, 49). Leopardi knew nothing of Hegelian philosophy, but his hostility to dialectics, which he associated with teleology and narratives of progress, would be crucial to later ways of reading his work as an encounter with the political. As Timpanaro noted rather tartly, for Leopardi 'unhappiness is not to be "dialecticized" away at the level of logic' (49).

Timpanaro may have been heavily invested in the 'battle for Leopardi', but he was careful not to claim the poet as a kind of 'pre-Marxist' thinker, arguing elsewhere that his pessimism is important precisely as an instance of 'that which isn't in Marx and others' (Timpanaro, 1985, 196). Much of this, of course, seems to fly in the face of the poet's own expressed lack of interest in politics, but in understanding pessimism as just one dimension of a more complex scepticism it situates the political within the purview of the imagination: 'I detest politics', Leopardi writes, because I believe, or rather I see, that individuals are unhappy under any form of government; the fault is nature's, which made men for unhappiness; and I laugh at the happiness of the *masses*, because my small brain can't conceive of a happy *mass* made up of individuals who are not happy. (1998, 252)

Leopardi's 'liquidation of the world of politics', in Antonio Negri's phrase (2015, 206), might sound frivolous, but it already contains the germ of a dissociation that has become very familiar in recent political thinking – a dissociation between 'politics' and 'the political'. This so-called political difference, modelled on Heidegger's ontological distinction between 'beings' and 'Being', figures 'politics' as the domain of decision and position, while 'the political' reserves to itself, in Esposito's words, 'the space of a form of thinking from where alone, by contrast, the sphere of politics could be thought' (qtd in Bosteels, 2011, 106). Christopher Fynsk (1991, x) defines 'the political' as 'the site where what it means to *be* in common is open to definition' (his emphasis) while 'politics' consists in 'the play of forces and interests engaged in a conflict over the representation and governance of social existence'. Timpanaro is helpful again in clarifying how 'the political' expresses a strong ontological element ('what it means to *be* in common', in Fynsk's phrase): while Leopardi's early pessimism seems privately motivated and rooted in personal suffering, after his physical and mental breakdown in 1819 the poet came increasingly to see unhappiness as the determining condition of all living beings. And this is not just a kind of vague existentialist *angst* but, as Timpanaro emphasises, 'a physical unhappiness based on highly concrete givens: illness, old age, the ephemerality of pleasure' (Timpanaro, 1979, 38), hence Leopardi's later criticism of those who 'have wished to consider my philosophical opinions as the result of my personal suffering, and persist in attributing to my material circumstances what is due solely to my understanding' (Leopardi, 1998, 263).

Timpanaro thus attributes to Leopardi what he calls a 'pessimistic materialism' and this seems a helpful way of defining what he shares with Beckett, a pessimism that is not reducible to subjectivism and metaphysics but that is rooted instead in the travails of the body. This 'site', as Fynsk terms it, or *mise-en-scène*, is framed, of course, by philosophical concepts, and here again we should heed Nietzsche's call for 'absolute scepticism' towards an inherited vocabulary. This can lead to the creation of new concepts – the 'unpolitical', the 'impolitical' and so on – but also to the related elaboration of forms of negative or sceptical thinking that draw their resources more from literature and *poesis* than from philosophy, that expose the latter's principal concepts to the play of contingency and relativism that Nietzsche had taken to characterise the contents excluded from conventional philosophical thinking (Esposito, 2012,

11–12). It was precisely for this reason that Leopardi, in some respects a notably romantic poet, found himself attacking Italy's new Romantic writers who, he claims,

> wish to make poetry consort with the intellect, and to transplant it from the visible to the invisible, and from things to ideas, and to transform it from the material, imaginative, corporeal substance that it was into something metaphysical, reasonable and spiritual. (Leopardi, 2013b, 115)

The distinction between philosophy and poetry – they are 'enemies', Leopardi says elsewhere (Z1650) – is a consistent strand in his thinking: much later he writes that 'the more philosophical poetry is, the less poetical it is', and that 'Literature, and especially poetry, has nothing to do with subtle, rigorous, and precise philosophy, for it has the beautiful as its object, which is as much as to say the false, because the true (since man's sad fate requires it) was never beautiful' (Z1228).

It is not, however, simply a matter of literature offering a counter to philosophy, of its pitting a language of sensory immediacy against one of 'cold' abstraction; nor is it a matter of using poems simply to issue propositions of a sceptical kind. Leopardi's insight is rather that a materialist poetics will grasp scepticism as its own formal and ontological necessity, as the very condition of its self-reflexive insistence. A poetics of this kind openly avows its own status as illusion rather than as truth. As Leopardi says in his polemic against Romanticism, 'one may beguile in such a way that the people experience the delight which is the purpose of poetry, benefiting from the fiction but not believing it except in imagination, and thus without harm' (Leopardi, 2013b, 119). This refusal of any reassuring 'ground' would lead Leopardi to a poetics of sceptical 'abandonment' and exposure that significantly prefigures the later art of Beckett.

While 'lucidity' might seem a recognisably eighteenth-century virtue, Leopardi was ambivalent about the claims of Enlightenment thought, admiring its way of striking down 'false' superstitions (the belief in an afterlife, for example), but at the same time regretting its tendency to undermine those beliefs or illusions that he considered were still needed to make our lives supportable (beauty, happiness and so on). As Esposito observes (2012, 124), the poet reacts by working to 'superimpose illusion and reason – in other words [...] to recognize the illusory nature of illusion by turning a once spontaneous fiction into a conscious fiction'. Leopardi, he contends (126), develops a theory of the imagination as something not opposed to reason but existing as its 'indispensable, internal structure'. As Leopardi puts it, 'Reason needs the imagination and the illusions that reason destroys' (Z1839). And so, we might add, does reason need poetry, for it is in poetry's acknowledgement of its own fictiveness that what Nietzsche had seen as the repressed contents of philosophical thinking may return, thus (in Esposito's words) 'recognizing in the sovereign power of death the pulsing of a life that it cannot entirely eliminate because it constitutes the matter, so to speak, without which death would not be what it is' (Esposito, 2012, 128). What Esposito terms 'the pulsing of a life' expresses for Leopardi the very essence of the aesthetic – not as some sort of vitalist enthusiasm but as a paradox that signifies only in its relentless self-expression as the force of existence. As he puts it in the 'Dialogue between Nature and an Icelander', 'in this universe life is a perpetual cycle of production and destruction' (Leopardi, 1982, 199).

To regard Leopardi and Beckett as simply pessimists is to miss the complexity of this 'cycle' that recasts politics as a play of forces rather than of values. Both rail against the deadly grip of 'habit', and both accordingly value writing as (in Leopardi's words) 'a continuous and uninterrupted activity, vivacity, and freshness of imagination' (Z3718–19). Persistence, we might say, implies a pessimism that won't quite accept its own claim to absoluteness, so while great works of art often seem to 'treat and represent nothing but death', in doing so they may also 'restore, albeit momentarily, the life that it [the soul] had lost' (Z260). It is through the vividness ['vivacità'] of the aesthetic effect that 'the soul receives life (if only fleetingly) from the very force with which it feels the perpetual death of things, and its own death' (Z261). Contradictions abound, amongst which perhaps this one takes primacy, that Leopardi cannot 'reconcile the power of human imagination and feeling with the frailty of the human body and the transience of human beauty' (Williams, 2004, 95). Such contradictions provide, ironically, a sort of ground, the only one, perhaps, that 'absolute scepticism' can allow, though, as Leopardi observes,

> that principle [of non-contradiction], which once rooted out puts an end to every discourse, every line of reasoning, every proposition, and the very faculty we have through them to form and conceive of truths, that fundamental principle 'A thing cannot both be and not be' seems absolutely false when you consider the palpable contradictions there are in nature. (Z4099)

Such contradictions fly in the face of Aristotelian logic, then, but for the lucid eye they are plain to see in 'nature' where the apparently antithetical relation of life to death, of creation to destruction, conceals the fact that, as we shall see throughout this Element, they are always intimately entwined, parts of a single process. The desire for happiness, for example, is found in everybody, but this desire is naturally insatiable and thus can only be the cause of unhappiness (Citati, 2016, 250).

If contradiction brings 'discourse' to a standstill, then, we shall perhaps look to poetry to grasp that contradictoriness not as something anomalous and exceptional but as a constitutive feature of lived experience. Leopardi, of course, thinks of poetry in these terms because it is in poetry that language becomes doubtful, offering a means of undoing 'the purported perfecting of reason and of philosophy' that, he says, 'the system of things favours' (Z1839). What 'the system of things' does not 'favour', though, is precisely the kind of sceptical force that Leopardi will derive from the poetic; in contrast, the Romantic poets, he claims, won't ruffle any feathers because already they are stripping poetry of 'its basic capacity to fictionalize and to beguile', thus facilitating its assimilation to metaphysics (Leopardi, 2013b, 116). Language, then, is clearly the contested terrain, and Leopardi develops his argument through what has become a well-known distinction between 'words' ('parole') and 'terms' ('termini'). 'In the sciences', he says, 'precise words are appropriate and good, but in literature it is the right words' that count (Z1226). 'Each is exactly the opposite of the other', and where the sciences use words with 'dry, bare meanings', the poet seeks out 'words that are vaguer and express more uncertain ideas, or a greater number of ideas, etc.'. Just as Leopardi emphasises that illusions are fictions that we have made ourselves – they are 'second nature', not some gift from beyond – so the poet's words should share with 'ancient words' a rootedness in 'the material and sensible' (Z1704); here speaks the poet as philologist, of course, but a philologist for whom the ancient languages can enliven 'the modern dryness' with what he calls their 'freshness, color, softness, brilliance, *embonpoint* [plumpness], richness, vigor, etc.' (Z111).

'Vagueness', then, is the protection poetry offers against the generalising 'dryness' of the concept; Beckett's rejection of Cartesian 'clarity' runs along similar lines, resulting in the injunction to himself when writing *Happy Days* to 'vaguen it' (qtd in de la Durantaye, 2016, 85). Paradoxically, perhaps, it is poetry's immersion in the 'material and sensible' that makes its language ripe with semantic reversals, with a kind of negative knowledge of familiar concepts, as truth and falsehood, reality and illusion slip their moorings to change places, and poems come to pivot around negative paradoxes and oxymorons like 'blissful error', 'unhappy truth' – 'this paradoxical figure of speech is absolutely intrinsic to [Leopardi's] system of thought', says Pamela Williams (2004, 65). Through poetry, then (and, in Beckett's case, poetry rendered as prose, and as drama), we may think while knowing that our thinking has no ultimate ground: 'all truths', says Leopardi, 'have two different or opposed aspects, indeed, an infinite number of them [...] no truth or falsehood is absolute' (Z1632). Doubt and uncertainty thus become the very measure of a kind of thinking that will entertain what reason will not. What is more, this thinking is, as already noted, intimately bound up with reason itself. So Leopardi writes:

> My system introduces a Skepticism that is not only reasoned and proven, but is such that human reason, according to my system, whatever possible progress is made, will never succeed in ridding itself of this skepticism. On the contrary, it contains the truth, and it is demonstrated that our reason can absolutely not find the truth save by doubting, that it distances itself from truth whenever it judges with certainty, and that not only does doubt serve to uncover the truth [...] but that truth essentially consists in doubt, and whoever doubts knows, and knows as much as one can know. (Z1655)

The piling up of paradoxes in this passage strews the argument with obstacles, dissolving truth and knowledge in doubt and blocking the way to the kind of generality and 'certainty' we expect of the concept. 'Whoever doubts knows, and knows as much as one can know': Leopardi thus sets a limit to Enlightenment ambition and in so doing situates knowledge on the uncertain terrain of a poetic thinking that enacts the constant oscillation between affirmation and negation that immersion in 'the material and sensible' seems to dictate. We have what Bruno Clément (1994, 48) has called, after Beckett, 'A Rhetoric of Ill-Saying', a rhetoric which is concerned not so much with persuasion as with language's capacity to doubt itself, to retract its own statements and to demonstrate over and over that the more that is said, the less is revealed.

For Beckett, then, as for Leopardi, the only 'ground' to which we can appeal is that of experience, the shifting, literal 'mud' of life itself whose contingency ever denies us a secure footing. This is a world replete with illusion and contradiction, a 'region' (to use Beckett's word) where one finds oneself 'talking about things that do not exist, or that exist perhaps, impossible to know, beside the point' (Beckett, 1994, 307). *The Unnamable*, the title of the novel from which that passage is drawn, typifies this paradox or aporia, invoking an act of nomination that even as it pointlessly names someone who cannot be named must nonetheless be endlessly repeated. Indeed, this text begins by associating aporia with this kind of persistence: 'What am I to do, what shall I do, what should I do, in my situation, how proceed? By aporia pure and simple? Or by affirmations and negations invalidated as uttered, or sooner or later?' (293). This scepticism about the effectiveness of language – a scepticism for which Beckett found confirmation in the theoretical writings of Fritz Mauthner (see Ben-Zvi, 1980) – leads not to some eventual certainty but to a kind of endless unravelling of conceptual ambitions that can finally express only persistence itself, a persistence that is not an effort to overcome contradiction but rather a determination to 'go on' in the face of contradiction, acknowledging this as the primary condition of existence. For Beckett, this persistence would find its exemplary expression in the indefatigable beating heart of Leopardi's 'To Himself'.

2 The Beating Heart: 'To Himself'

To explain Beckett's fascination with 'To Himself' solely in terms of his youthful pessimism is, however, to miss what would prove to be an altogether deeper engagement with the complex questions of being and non-being raised by Leopardi's poem. Did Beckett already discern a deeper intellectual current in this 'gloomy composition'? The question is worth asking because the poem has long divided critical opinion. Benedetto Croce (1943, 380–3), for example, was predictably dismissive of it, regretting its author's departure from the richer lyric tones of his 'idylls'. Walter Binni (1947), however, valued it precisely for what he called its 'anti-idyllic' qualities and took it to represent a decisively new direction in the poet's work. Other critics such as Angelo Monteverdi drew attention to the deliberate artistry that lay behind Leopardi's 'icy' style in his late work, a style that, as we have noted, Croce (1923) dismissed as sententious ('gnomico') and essentially unpoetic ('non-poesia'). One way of explaining the importance Beckett attached to this poem is that he too saw it as marking a pivotal phase in Leopardi's career when the poet's negativity acquired such absoluteness that a new kind of style momentarily emerged.

'To Himself' was probably written in spring 1833 (Leopardi, 2021, 157) and is one of a group of poems known as the 'canti fiorentini' that include 'The Dominant Idea', 'Love and Death', 'Consalvo' and the slightly later 'Aspasia' (1834). Leopardi was resident in Florence from 23 March 1832 to 2 September 1833 when he and his friend Antonio Ranieri left for Naples. It was the period of the poet's passionate but unrequited attachment to Fanny Targioni Tozzetti, an emotional episode that deeply marked the poetry he wrote at this time. Indeed, the dark mood of 'To Himself' testifies to the failure not just of those romantic hopes but of hope in any form:

> Or poserai per sempre,
> Stanco mio cor. Perì l'inganno estremo,
> Ch'eterno io mi credei. Perì. Ben sento,
> In noi di cari inganni,
> Non che la speme, il desiderio è spento.   5
> Posa per sempre. Assai
> Palpitasti. Non val cosa nessuna
> I moti tuoi, nè di sospiri è degna

> La terra. Amaro e noia
> La vita, altro mai nulla; e fango è il mondo.   10
> T'acqueta omai. Dispera
> L'ultima volta. Al gener nostro il fato
> Non donò che il morire. Omai disprezza
> Te, la natura, il brutto
> Poter che, ascoso, a comun danno impera,   15
> E l'infinita vanità del tutto.
>
>   (Leopardi, 1987, 102)

> Now you may rest forever, worn-out heart.
> The last illusion, which I once believed
> Eternal, now is dead. It's dead. I sense
> Not only hope but even the desire
> For sweet illusions is now spent in us.
> Be still forever, heart. You've beaten long
> Enough. Not anything at all is worth
> Your throbbing, nor does earth deserve your sighs.
> Boredom and bitterness is what life is
> And nothing more. The world is merely mud.
> Do not despair, or if you must despair,
> Succumb one final time. Fate gave our kind
> No gift but death. Nature, henceforth disdain
> Yourself – brute, hidden power that ordains
> Our pain, the common doom, the infinite
> Vanity of all existing things.

Something previously taken to be 'eternal' – the illusion ('l'inganno') of romantic love – has 'died'. In the earlier 'idylls', Leopardi had looked back fondly to the innocent 'illusions' of childhood and antiquity to rediscover the apparently unmediated experiences that could make humanity's lot seem a happy one. The modern world, however, is defined by what he called in 'To Silvia' (1828) the 'appearance of truth' ('All'apparir del vero'), which spells the death of such aesthetic 'illusions'. In 'To Himself', the emphatic past tense of the repeated 'Perì' ('it died') in lines 2 and 3 combine with the poem's opening conjunction of 'now' ('Or') and 'always' ('sempre') to emphasise the finality of this 'death'. Leopardi mourns the passing not only of hope but of desire itself. The language here is the 'most naked, broken and laconic' of any of Leopardi's works, says Mario Andrea Rigoni (Leopardi, 1987, 97), and other critics have remarked on the uncharacteristic 'hammering' ['martellatura'] effect of the poem's rhythm (Lonardi, 1989, 29). Indeed, as Angelo Monteverdi (1967, 127) observed in his influential reading of the poem, it contains hardly a line that is not subjected to some syntactical fragmentation, with propositions standing alone, shorn of connecting conjunctions and often broken across two lines (see, for example, lines 6–10). 'It rarely happens', says Monteverdi (129), 'that the syntactical phrase coincides with the rhythmic phrase'. 'To Himself' mixes eleven- and seven-syllable lines as Leopardi so frequently does, but, as Monteverdi also notes, these are sometimes decomposed so that the septenary 'il desiderio è spento', for example, appears as just part of line 5, while the hendecasyllabic 'Non val cosa nessuna / I moti tuoi' is only half-heard as it is enjambed across lines 7 and 8. The resulting discordance is even more striking when verbs are withheld (as in 'Amaro e noia / La vita', lines 9–10), an effect that creates an abrupt yoking together of words that receives additional emphasis from Leopardi's percussive punctuation (as, for example, in the use of comma, semicolon and full stops in lines 10–11). 'To Himself' employs twelve full stops in just sixteen lines (Rota, 1996, 198) and enjambement is more prominent than in any other poem by Leopardi (Monteverdi, 1967, 129).

This might seem, as it did to Croce, a severely disfigured style when compared to the fluent melodies of the earlier poems. Certainly, it is one that forgoes the consolations of the lyric mode and deploys the poet's address to himself less as a means of personal meditation than as the vehicle of a vengeful irony. Leopardi's dialogue of self and heart in 'To Himself' is modelled on the stoic *Meditations* of Marcus Aurelius (Leopardi, 1988, 1216), a book written in Greek and originally called *Eis heauton* (*To Himself*). Leopardi had once planned to write a 'practical' guide to life with the same title, and he had also translated the *Encheiridion* or *Manual* of Epictetus, whose disciple Marcus had been (see D'Intino, 2012, 152–76). Originally, it seemed to Leopardi that these ancient writers were able to interrogate the self without falling into the trap of egoism that lay in wait for the meditative philosopher of modernity (his example was the 'philosopher-prince' Frederick II; see Z2292–5). Leopardi's interest in the Stoics soon waned, however, and when he returned to Marcus's title in 'To Himself', it was with a sharpened sense of the error of assuming that 'the wise man [...] is in no regard subject to fortune' (Z2801). In Leopardi's hands, Marcus's 'speaking to himself, and about himself, that is about his heart, etc. (not about his public affairs, as Cicero does)' (Z2168) expresses a turbulence and a frustration that are remote indeed from the measured and engaging tone of the *Meditations*. 'To Himself' is hardly, then, a celebration of Stoic *ataraxia*; while the poet instructs his heart to quieten down ('T'acqueta mai', line 11), the Leopardian subject is characteristically 'restless' ['inquieto'], and 'anything but firmly anchored to a center' (Benvenuti, 1998, 131), while the poem's depiction of nature's 'brute, hidden power' (lines 14–15) starkly disputes Marcus's harmonious sense of 'The world as a living being – one nature, one soul' (Marcus Aurelius, 2002, 82).

Leopardi's version of Marcus's intimate dialogue retains his original's use of imperatives to address himself (Lonardi, 1989, 26), but this self is very different from the ancient one. With the 'death' of illusions, it is as if modern philosophy has triumphed over poetry, replacing the 'natural' and spontaneous self of the ancients with one that is mired in self-consciousness. As Leopardi writes in his *Zibaldone*, it is the social nature of modern life that is responsible for inducing man 'to reflect on himself' and to cultivate the meditative rather than the practical life (Z2684). In another passage of self-criticism, he avows that 'My mistake has been in wanting to lead a life which is all and entirely internal, with the aim and hope of finding peace' (Z4259; see Benvenuti, 1998, 130–3) . So in 'To Himself' the poet berates his heart for continuing to beat because 'your throbbing' ('I moti tuoi') is the very sign of the continuance of desire and of self-consciousness. For the reader who recalls Leopardi's early poems, there is dark irony here, for the quickened heartbeat had once signalled the advent of passion, inciting the poet in 'Il primo amore' ('First Love', 1817) to address his heart in an extended apostrophe ('Tell me now, tender heart'), and while those lines express pain and confusion, there is also consolation to be had from the beloved's image that remains with him. 'To Himself' returns to this trope of the beating heart, but where in the earlier poem the heart is 'fortemente palpitando' (line 21), here its motion bespeaks only exhaustion ('Stanco mio cor') and despair (lines 2, 11). The late poem inverts the figure of the heart's awakening, making it now an expression of failing life. Beckett clearly found in this poem, and in the accumulated woe of Leopardi's protracted ill-health, an echo of his own struggles with (as he described his symptoms to his therapist, Wilfred Bion) 'a bursting, apparently arrhythmic heart, night sweats, shudders, panic, breathlessness, and, when his condition was at its most severe, total paralysis' (Knowlson, 1996, 169). Leopardi's letters and autobiographical comments show how many of these disturbing symptoms also afflicted him (for his recurring 'terrori notturni' [night terrors], see Leopardi, 1988, 721–2). In Beckett's case, the problem of his 'bitch of a heart' (Beckett, 2009, 69) regularly surfaced in his early work: in *Proust*, for example, he associates his subject's style with 'fatigue of the heart, a blood fatigue' (88), while *Dream* spoke of the vicissitudes of 'his little heart' (1992a, 140) and *The Unnamable* worried about 'his heart [...] on its waltz, in his ear' (1994, 366). *The Calmative* would emphasise the non-figurative use of this organ with talk of its 'great red lapses' (1995, 51).

As we shall see in Section 3, Leopardi and Beckett share a habit of doubtful thinking that constantly confronts the contradictory nature of experience that the ambiguous character of the beating heart seems powerfully to express. For while the heart's action is the very guarantee of continuing vitality, its pounding motion can also seem to threaten the body's health and stability. This constant sense of imminent death produces, says Leopardi, a sort of 'hatred of the self' (Z619) and several years later he has this to say about the young man (himself, of course) who 'for whatever reason [...] is spurned by the world':

> He becomes misanthropic toward himself and is his own worst enemy, he wants to suffer, he persists in wanting to suffer [...] and if he has to find a state, then the most monotonous, the coldest, the most painful because of the boredom it brings, the most difficult to bear because it is the furthest away from life and participates least in it, is the one which he prefers. (Z3838)

This terrible description of the young man deliberately 'turning himself to ice' will issue later in the cold, 'naked' style of 'To Himself', a style that strives to petrify the speaker's own beating heart. The intimate conversation with the self here leads not to some private serenity but to a self-estrangement in which interiority is reified as a mechanical object ('Non val cosa nessuna / I moti tuoi', 'Not anything at all is worth / Your throbbing', lines 7–8). The way of addressing the self as 'you' is no longer, as it was for Marcus Aurelius, the vocative of a spiritual exercise but an acknowledgement, rather, that 'spirit' itself has become alien and objectified.

When Leopardi made his translation of Epictetus's *Manual* late in 1825, he acknowledged in his introduction the help it had given him in a troubled period of his life (Leopardi, 1988, 1047). To a young man with unbounded ambition, the philosopher offered a bracing sense of the limits to human power:

> Some things are within our power, while others are not. Within our power are opinion, motivation, desire, aversion, and, in a word, whatever is of our own doing; not within our power are our body, our property, reputation, office, and, in a word, whatever is not of our own doing. (Epictetus, 2014, 296)

As the grim tone of 'To Himself' demonstrates, however, Leopardi would later see those things such as 'desire', which Epictetus had declared to be within our own 'power', as increasingly expressive of some other 'brute, hidden power that 'ordains / Our pain, the common doom' (lines 14–15). With humanity thus revealed as the plaything of fate or nature, stoic serenity is eclipsed by a defiant black humour that, as in the poem 'Aspasia', might seem to offer revenge ('vendetta') on the feckless Fanny but actually does nothing to free the poet from his torpid condition (in the closing lines of 'Aspasia', he imagines himself prone and unmoving beneath an indifferent sky but smiling darkly nonetheless). In a curious foreshadowing of a familiar Beckettian trope, the speaker's 'immobility' here recalls *Dream*'s Belacqua, with his 'head in his thighs', inhabiting 'a Limbo from which the mistral of desire had been withdrawn' (Beckett, 1992a, 66).

The same embittered sense of absurdity increasingly infects Leopardi's handling of Stoic tropes. In the *Zibaldone*, for example, he writes:

> What is life? The journey of a crippled and sick man walking with a heavy load on his back up steep mountains and through wild, rugged, arduous places, in snow, ice, rain, wind, burning sun, for many days without ever resting night and day to end at a precipice or ditch, in which inevitably he falls. (Z4162–3)

In this 1826 notebook entry, Leopardi deliberately reverses the Stoic trope of the 'path of life', as that is developed, for example, by Seneca:

> The first part only has rocks and cliffs, and appears impassable, just as many places, when viewed from afar, seem often to be an unbroken steep since the distance deceives the eye; then, as you draw nearer, these same places, which by a trick of the eyes had merged into one, open up gradually, and what seemed from a distance precipitous is now reduced to a gentle slope. (Z4163, editorial note)

Leopardi's rewriting of this journey as a narrative of torment and exposure predicts the figures of constant, pointless movement in Beckett's fiction and the related dream there of a silent immobility. The gentle slope of Seneca's path becomes in Leopardi's version a ditch into which the crippled man must 'inevitably' fall and the bitter tone here is of a piece with Beckett's image of humanity 'lashed to the stake, blindfold, gagged to the gullet' (Beckett, 1994, 396). Not surprisingly, Beckett often alludes to Leopardi's poem 'Night Song of a Wandering Shepherd in Asia', where the tale of the 'little old white-haired man' is told again, this time with him falling not into a precipice or ditch (as we shall later see Molloy do) but into 'a horrible, immense abyss'. Beckett clearly appreciated both the inhospitability of the poem's moonlit landscape and Leopardi's reluctance to have this story of doomed persistence deliver a Bunyanesque moral allegory.

The first lines of 'To Himself' also echo the opening of Ugo Foscolo's 1802 sonnet similarly titled 'Of Himself' ('Di se stesso'): 'Non son chi fui—perì di noi gran parte: / questo che avanza è sol languore e pianto' ('I am not what I was – so much is lost: / Nothing remains but to lament and weep'; Foscolo, 2009, 6–7). Loss and decline are echoed in Leopardi's own twice repeated 'perì' ('it died'), while a phrase in his poem's second line – 'Stanco mio cor' – complicates the allusion to Foscolo's poem by also recalling Petrarch's 'Mira quell colle, o stanco mio cor vago' ('Look at that hill, my tired heart that yearns'; Petrarch, 1996, 346), so initiating a series of references to fatigue and exhaustion that will later permeate Beckett's work. This fatigue is the measure of time itself, of 'those interminable intervals of time during which', says

Leopardi, 'existence is duration rather than life' (Leopardi, 1982, 165). Such exhaustion leaves the heart almost too tired to continue beating – 'Assai / Palpitasti' ('You've beaten long / Enough', lines 6–7), he writes, with the enjambement palpably expressing the speaker's weariness. But even with the promise of death to free us from this unrelenting rhythm (lines 12–13), the temporal moment of the poem is a contradictory one. We are told that 'now' the heart *will* rest forever ('or poserai'), but the confident future tense gives way to a series of wishful imperatives ('Posa per sempre', 'T'acqueta omai', 'Dispera / L'ultima volta') that only further emphasise the deferral of the much longed for state of rest or non-being. The heart is exhausted, then, but it still isn't dead and, as Pietro Citati notes (2016, 384), 'it won't therefore stop desiring, beating, moving, breathing. It doesn't want to quieten down'. This indomitable will to live is non-productive, though, a stamina with no redeeming moral value and thoroughly tainted by the 'sterility' of boredom (see Z1815). This negative aspect of persistence is closely attuned to the famous ending of Beckett's *The Unnamable* (Beckett, 1995, 418): 'in the silence you don't know, you must go on, I can't go on, I'll go on'.

Until this late stage, Leopardi had always scorned a language of 'nude parole' ('bare words') or what he calls in the distinction we have already quoted 'termini' as opposed to 'parole'. Where the sciences use words with 'dry, bare meanings' ('voci di nudo e secco significato'; Z109), the poet seeks out 'words that are vaguer and express more uncertain ideas, or a greater number of ideas, etc.' (Z1226). Leopardi's early poetry eschews the 'naked' truths of philosophy in an effort to recover those illusions that we know to be illusions; in his later years, though, he ceases to advocate illusions as compensatory fictions, and his poetry will find itself compelled to confront its own 'nakedness', just as the fall of Adam and Eve was 'occasioned by knowledge, in that man *knew* what he had not known before, and would not and should not have known, namely that he was naked' (Z399; emphasis in original). Perhaps this frightening nakedness and exposure had constituted the real horizon of Leopardi's poetics all along; certainly, his understanding of them as distinctive features of the modern sensibility is comparable to what Walter Benjamin says of artists like Paul Klee and Adolf Loos, that 'both reject the traditional, solemn, noble image of man, festooned with all the sacrificial offerings of the past. They turn instead to the naked man of the contemporary world who lies screaming like a newborn babe in the dirty diapers of the present' (Benjamin, 1999, 733).

Leopardi and Beckett both impugn this 'noble image of man', the former by his move from a Stoic care of the self towards a vengeful pessimism, the latter by beginning where Leopardi seems to end, with the 'icy' disillusion of 'To Himself'. As early as *Proust*, Beckett was dismissive of 'our smug will to live, of our pernicious and incurable optimism' (1965, 15), and by 1936 he was attempting to salvage something from the remains of Stoicism as he rediscovered them in the *Ethics* of the seventeenth-century Belgian philosopher Arnold Geulincx. Beckett's reading of Geulincx concentrates on one sentence and a small number of images that will reappear in his fiction (see Beckett, 2011, 149–50). The sentence 'Ubi nihil vales, ibi nihil velis' is variously translated as 'Where one is worth nothing, one should want nothing' and 'Wherein you have no power, therein neither should you will'.[8] For Geulincx as a Christian theologian, of course, everything that lies outside us is for God to determine. The *Ethics* counsels humility above all and a certain disregard of self: 'we learn by inspecting ourselves that we can do nothing about any part of the human condition, we have no power, and no rights over it; that it is all down to someone else's power' (Geulincx, 2006, 327). Geulincx concludes that 'I do nothing outside myself; that whatever I do stays within me', and in Beckett's notes on the *Ethics*, he observes that Geulincx hereby 'reduces self-activity to immanent mental activity in man' (qtd in Tucker, 2012, 23). Here, then, is one antidote to the peculiar vanity that conceives of humans as the determining centre of the world; the vanity that means that, as Leopardi puts it (1982, 433), 'We consider, and shall always consider, ourselves the first and the supremely important among all earthly creatures'. Against such vanity, Geulincx (2006, 333) avows that 'I am a mere spectator of a machine whose workings I can neither adjust nor readjust. I neither construct nor demolish anything here: the whole thing is someone else's affair'.

This passivity is bought at a price, however, and while in Geulincx's own case this is joyously and humbly paid, for the secular Leopardi and Beckett the limits set to the self's power can also make the human world seem a straitened place. Leopardi had already observed in the early poem 'To Angelo Mai' that 'the world when once known doesn't expand: it shrinks', and Beckett borrowed his own image of existential limitation from another passage in Geulincx's *Ethics*:

> a ship carrying a passenger with all speed towards the west in no way prevents the passenger from walking towards the east [...] so the will of God, carrying all things, impelling all things with memorable force, in no way prevents us from resisting his will (as much as in our power) with complete freedom. (Geulincx, 2006, 317)

The ship reappears in *Molloy* as 'the black boat of Ulysses' (Beckett, 1994, 51), and in answer to a query from his German translator Beckett provided a gloss:

---

[8] Quigley contends that 'both translations of Geulincx's maxims insert "should", whereas a more felicitous translation would simply be "wherein you can do nothing, therein you will nothing"' (2024, 105).

'I imagine a member of the crew who does not share the adventurous spirit of Ulysses and is at least at liberty to crawl homewards (nach Osten) along the brief deck' (Beckett, 2011, 458). The voracious desire for knowledge and power that drives Ulysses' Western adventure ends in shipwreck off the Pillars of Hercules; like Leopardi, though, Beckett is concerned not with epic heroes but with 'a few little animals that live on a handful of mud' (Leopardi, 1982, 417–19), and where the Greek ship plunges boldly on into the unknown, Beckett's sailor (initially a mere 'galley-man' in *The Unnamable*, but later freed from 'the shadow of the lash'; Beckett, 1994, 396) exploits what little freedom he has to 'crawl homewards', though any progress he might make along the 'brief' deck is immediately cancelled by the craft's headlong dash in the opposite direction, 'nach Westen'. That contradictory and constraining space would be the *mise-en-scène* of Beckett's work to come.

3 Voices of the Dead: Leopardi's 'Chorus'

In 'To Himself', the heart that continues to beat provides Leopardi's most dramatic image of the endless struggle between existential constraint and human persistence, and it is not hard to see why the poem was so important to Beckett. But here we want to suggest that an earlier work that in some ways prefigured 'To Himself' may also have had a significant effect on this aspect of Beckett's thinking. This is the remarkable 'Chorus of the Dead' which introduces the prose 'Dialogue between Frederick Ruysch and His Mummies', written in 1824 and included in the *Operette morali* published that year (Leopardi, 1982, 270–83). While 'To Himself' stages a bitter contest between the self that longs for peace and the heart that will not give up living, the 'Chorus' seems to grasp the dilemma of existence – impossibly – from the other side of death itself. Leopardi's 'Dialogue' alludes to the ancient view that 'the universe followed an orbit, which brought it back to the starting point; the time needed for such a revolution was called the "great" or "mathematical" year' (Leopardi, 1982, 526 n.2). At the end of such a cycle, many thousands of normal years long, apocalyptic events were expected to take place. Here the legions of the dead are given the opportunity to speak for a quarter of an hour if addressed by a living person. But first they sing, and readers have much admired their stately chorus – in 1905 James Thomson praised it as 'one of the marvels of literature' (Thomson, 1905, 204); more recently Michel Orcel (2005) has called it 'one of the finest and most troubling works of its period' (328). Orcel, like fellow translator Jonathan Galassi (Leopardi, 2010), acknowledges its power by presenting it as a free-standing poem. As we noted earlier, Beckett's edition of the *Canti*, quite unusually for its time, also presented the 'Chorus' in this way, which may have drawn his attention to it (Leopardi, 1936, 249–50). The poem also uncannily prefigures aspects of the later 'To Himself', most notably in its fragmented rhythms, its emphatic enjambements and its double negation of hope and desire (the connection is noted in Vecce, 2000, 26, and Rota, 1996, 201).

> Sola nel mondo eterna, a cui si volve
> Ogni creata cosa,
> In te, morte, si posa
> Nostra ignuda natura;
> Lieta no, ma sicura   5
> Dall'antico dolor. Profonda notte
> Nella confusa mente
> Il pensier grave oscura;
> Alla speme, al desio, l'arido spirto
> Lena mancar sì sente: 10
> Così d'affanno e di temenza è sciolto,
> E l'età vote e lente
> Senza tedio consuma.
> Vivemmo: e qual di paurosa larva,
> E di sudato sogno,   15
> A lattante fanciullo erra nell'alma
> Confusa ricordanza:
> Tal memoria n'avanza
> Del viver nostro: ma da tema è lunge
> Il rimembrar. Che fummo?   20
> Che fu quel punto acerbo
> Che di vita ebbe nome?
> Cosa arcana e stupenda
> Oggi è la vita al pensier nostro, e tale
> Qual de' vivi al pensiero   25
> L'ignota morte appar. Come da morte
> Vivendo rifuggia, così rifugge
> Dalla fiamma vitale
> Nostra ignuda natura;
> Lieta no ma sicura;   30
> Però ch'esser beato
> Nega ai mortali e nega a' morti il fato. (Leopardi, 1988, 116–17)

> Alone eternal
> In the world,
> Towards you, O Death,
> All beings turn –
> In you alone
> Our naked nature
> Finds repose,

Its final rest –
Happy, no,
But yet secure
From ancient suffering
And sorrow.

Deep night obscures
In our confused
And darkened minds
The heavy thought:
The dried-up spirit,
Lacking strength
For hope
And for desire,
No longer seeking
What it sought,
Is freed from fear,
Anxiety,
Consuming
Without tedium
The blank, slow ages
Of eternity.

We were alive,
And as the fearsome
Phantom
Of a nursing infant's
Feverish dream
Wanders within
Its soul
As a confused
And vaguely troubling
Memory,
So we remember
Our own lives;
But far from fear
Are we.

What were we then?
(What were we, then?)
What was that unripe
Moment with the name
Of life? What
Was its bitter point?
Stupendous and arcane
Is life now to our thought –
Just as to the living

> Death appears unknown.
> As, living, it shunned death,
> So now our naked nature
> Shuns the vital flame:
> Happy, no,
> But yet secure;
> For fate prohibits
> Happiness
> Both to the dead
> And those who, having breath,
> Are yet to suffer death.

Leopardi's interlocutor in the dialogue that follows the chorus is Frederick Ruysch, a seventeenth-century Dutch anatomist who invented a process of embalming which produced stunningly lifelike effects in the corpses he used – liquid white wax was injected into the blood vessels of the cadaver and then stained red after it cooled (Kooijmans, 2022, 14). The 'Mummies' were exhibited in Ruysch's studio, attracting, as Leopardi notes (1982, 273), visitors like Tsar Peter the Great who eventually purchased the whole collection and took it back to Russia. Ruysch was an exceptional technician, but he also had artistic aspirations and ornamented his corpses with baroque arrangements of stones and flowers and with quotations from the poets about the vanity of human life (see reproductions in Ebenstein, 2022). Leopardi, however, ignores Ruysch's impulse to point a moral, and the prose *operetta* begins with an abrupt shift of tone, introducing him as a sort of *commedia dell'arte* buffoon whose 'dialogue with the dead' rehearses lame conventional assumptions like 'the sensation of death is extremely painful' (Leopardi, 1982, 277) and it 'consists in the separation of the soul from the body' (279). The Mummy who responds to Ruysch declares him wrong on both counts, arguing that the passage into death is really like falling asleep and that it induces a 'languor' which is pleasurable 'as it frees man from greater suffering' (281). Leopardi had already explored analogies between dying and falling asleep in the *Zibaldone*, where he concluded that 'man (and any other animal) experiences a certain comfort, and therefore pleasure, in death' (Z291). A pleasure not unalloyed, perhaps, but like everything else in this dialogue not simply its opposite either; as the Chorus says, the dead are 'Happy, no, / But yet secure / From ancient suffering / And sorrow'; 'secure', that is, from the demands of hopeful existence and the desire for happiness. The 'ancient suffering', 'antico dolore' (line 6), is the burden of existence itself. The phrase echoes another that Leopardi uses several times in the *Canti*, 'antico errore', the 'error' of original sin but also of humanity's later obsession with 'truth' (Leopardi, 2019, 214, note to lines 11–21). Beckett seems to recall it when he talks of the 'old error' in *Echo's Bones* (Beckett, 2014a, 3) and of 'past passion, ancient error' in *Watt* (1976, 140). It is possible, too, that Leopardi's careful equivocation between happiness and 'security' ('Lieta no, ma sicura') prefigures Beckett's habit of self-interruption to qualify or to retract a previous statement. Think, for example, of *Watt*: 'No matter, he is content, No. Let us not exaggerate. He is well pleased. For he knows he is in the right place, at last' (39). Or of *Ohio Impromptu*: 'What thoughts who knows. Thoughts, no, not thoughts. Profounds of mind' (2006, 448). Those 'profounds of mind', that 'right place', with its promise of stillness, silence and sleep, are a constant object of desire for both our writers, making descriptive finality redundant. 'The place to be', writes Beckett in *The Unnamable*, is 'where you suffer, rejoice, at being bereft of speech, bereft of thought, and feel nothing, hear nothing, know nothing, say nothing, are nothing, that would be a blessed place to be, where you are' (1994, 377–8).

Leopardi's dialogue ends with a question from Ruysch to the Mummies that will remain unanswered: 'how did you know that you were dead?' (Leopardi, 1982, 283). The question meets only with a great silence which allows Ruysch to return gratefully to his bed, but which continues to resonate in readers' minds along with the still-echoing sounds of the Chorus. In that ringing silence we may realise how, with his assumption of an absolute separation between life and death, the anatomist has completely missed the point – for, as author of and participant in the 'Chorus of the Dead', and as the poet who only one year later would describe himself as a 'walking sepulchre' (Z4149), Leopardi knows with certainty that he at least is 'dead already'; 'I no longer see any difference between death and this life of mine', he had written to his friend and mentor Pietro Giordani, remarking, too, that, for most, 'life' never detaches itself from death's grip: 'the only people who live until they die are the many people who remain children all their lives' (Leopardi, 1998, 90, 91). As Pietro Citati observes (2016, 258–9), it is this recognition that entitles Leopardi to join the singers in the Chorus and provides an answer to Ruysch's final question: for to be a member of the Chorus is to find one's self now shrivelled and 'dried-up' ('l'arido spirito' of line 9 recalling Leopardi's earlier description of himself to Giordani as 'stiff and withered like a dry reed'; Leopardi, 1998, 95). The 'passage from being to non-being', as Leopardi calls it (Z293), with its 'ablation' of hope and desire (line 9), reduces the bodily self to a voice now 'pure' because all its vital attributes have been purged away (Fedi, 1997, 82). We may remember the fate of the nymph Echo, as told by Ovid and recalled by a youthful Beckett: 'Only her voice and her bones remain: then, only voice; for they say that her bones were turned to stone' (Ovid, 1971, 153). So when Leopardi describes human 'nature' as 'ignuda' ('naked'), he is, in the words of translator Geoffrey Bickersteth,

> not thinking here of spirit apart from body, but of the dead, without any distinction of soul and body, as 'naked,' that is, *stripped* of all thought, hope, desire, sensation and even of 'tedio' [tedium], as happens in profound and dreamless sleep, where there is no consciousness of time. (Bickersteth, 1923, 505 n.4; emphasis in original)

Bickersteth notes that most earlier commentators had taken 'ignuda' to mean 'disembodied', thus echoing Ruysch's own conventional belief in the separation of soul and body in death. Bickersteth, however, follows Giovanni Gentile (1918, 345) in taking Leopardi to mean that the dead retain the physical characteristics of the living while being 'deprived of life' and its attendant woes. The nakedness of Ruysch's Mummies, then, is that of their 'nature', which Leopardi thinks of in terms of a kind of 'non-being' that, it turns out, they share with the living who, like all created beings, are always already 'turning' towards death ('si volve', line 1). The upshot of this chiastic 'logic' is that, far from metamorphosing into pure spirit, the dead remain 'men asleep, ready to speak when they awake' (Leopardi, 1988, 1325).

The voices of the dead are heard also in many of Beckett's texts, early and late. We might think at least of *Dream* (Belacqua 'moved with the shades of the dead'; Beckett, 1992a, 44), *Echo's Bones* ('Belacqua is a human, dead and buried, restored to the jungle'; 2014a, 4), *Molloy* ('since I have ceased to live'; 1994, 25), *The Unnamable* ('I'm like dust, they want to make a man out of dust'; 351), *Endgame* ('Fit to wake the dead! Did you hear it?'; 2006, 115), *Company* ('On your back in the dark you remember'; 1992b, 31), *How It Is* ('warmth of primeval mud impenetrable dark'; 1996, 12), *Play* ('three identical grey urns'; 2006, 307), *The Calmative* ('No, it's not like me to come back to life, after my death'; 1995, 61), *Eh Joe* ('Mud thou art'; 2006, 365), *A Piece of Monologue* ('Birth was the death of him'; 425), *Rockaby* ('time she stopped'; 435), *What Where* ('I switch off'; 476) . . . . The list could go on, but Beckett had already encountered unsettling effects of the disembodied voice in his early reading of Proust: when the narrator receives a telephone call from his grandmother, 'he hears it now', says Beckett, 'for the first time, in all its purity and reality, so different from the voice that he had been accustomed to follow on the open score of her face that he does not recognize it as hers' (Beckett, 1965, 26–7). Suddenly unfamiliar, the voice is heard

> also as a symbol of her isolation, of their separation, as impalpable as a voice from the dead. The voice stops. His grandmother seems as irretrievably lost as Eurydice among the shades. Alone before the mouthpiece he calls her name in vain. (27)

There are intimations here of Krapp's dialogue with his own younger disembodied voice and of the minimalist presentation of Mouth in the later *Not I*. But Beckett's writing had always played host to 'All the dead voices', as Estragon calls them in *Waiting for Godot* (Beckett, 2006, 58), and often with disturbing results. For as the narrator's grandmother's voice is lost, so he too feels suddenly 'present at his own absence' ('he is not there because she does not know that he is there'; Beckett, 1965, 27); like a grief-stricken Orpheus, he is vainly calling his grandmother's name in the world of the shades. This is, to be sure, a realm into which the intrepid have occasionally ventured, though often to return with little compensation for the dangers of the journey (along with Orpheus we recall Odysseus, Juno, Heracles, Theseus and Aeneas). For Leopardi and Beckett, the descent into the 'primitive' underworld is an especially powerful figure when used to demonstrate that death brings with it no rewards or punishments. This is one of the points made in Leopardi's late political satire *Paralipomeni della Batrachomyomchia* (1830–7), mainly composed during his last years in Naples and providing a fictional 'supplement' to the pseudo-Homeric *Batrachomyomchia* he had translated three times in his youth. In the descent into Hades in Canto VIII of the satire, we are assured that 'Never did any savage have an inkling of rewards or punishment destined to the dead' (Leopardi, 1976, 102). This descent is a sort of failed *nekyia*, a voyage like that of a Geulingian 'galley-man, bound for the pillars of Hercules' and cursed by what Beckett calls in *The Unnamable* 'the mad wish to know' (Beckett, 1994, 339). As Leopardi drafted his epic poem, he might have recalled his own earlier excursion into the underworld in the 'Chorus of the Dead'. This time the inhabitants are animals – the poem tells of the *War of the Mice and the Crabs* – who perform another 'funereal chorus' ('quel funereo coro'; Leopardi, 1976, 103) as they sit in 'endless rows of seats', 'with their elongated and drowsy faces and their other members hanging and falling down'. This is no Dantean underworld of pain and punishment but one in which the dead are doomed to – or blessed with? – immobility, forgetfulness, indifference; 'No one looks at his neighbor or speaks to him' (103) and 'The deceased is not an animal who laughs' (104). This world is like that of Ruysch's Mummies where the dead do not converse because 'we wouldn't have anything to say to one another' (Leopardi, 1982, 275). Leopardi and Beckett would both have appreciated the ban on inconsequential chatter; indeed, the latter's own 'long sonata of the dead' memorialises the moment when 'the world dies too, foully named' and life falls victim to 'the well-built phrase' (Beckett, 1994, 31–2).

The 'Chorus of the Dead' is testimony to Leopardi's fascination with the function of the Chorus in ancient drama: 'the sound of its voice was not that of human individuals, it was a music, a harmony', he observed (Z2806). As the dead sing, the lyric voice of Leopardi's idylls suddenly becomes impersonal, a language of 'non-being' and negation liberated from the travails of existence to circulate around itself in a never-ending monotony. For Leopardi, some kind of outer limit of expression was arguably reached here, the limit marked by poetry's final lapse into silence as it confronts the unknowable and the unnamable, the 'stupendous and arcane' of line 23 (Giorni, 1988, 494). Except for the 'occasional' epistle to Carlo Pepoli (1826), the 'Chorus of the Dead' would be the last poem that Leopardi wrote until 'The Reawakening' four years later (Damiani, 1998, 236; De Robertis, 1986, 272). So, unexpectedly, poetry was abandoned for prose.

In its stately monotony, the 'Chorus' eschews the jagged movements of the later 'To Himself' but shares with it an intricate phonic patterning in which many of its words echo and rhyme with ones that follow: 'natura', 'sicura', 'dolor', 'sola', 'corsa', 'posa'; and these in turn are shadowed by the dark timbre of repeated /m/ sounds: 'mente', 'speme', 'temenze', 'Vivemmo', 'tema', 'rimembrar' (see Lonardi, 1982, 655–79). Domenico de Robertis (1986, 288) has said of Leopardi's composition that it is founded 'almost on a single note, held for a long time' with the slow monotone expressing the unchanging, timeless world of the dead. But it is also a world bound by the motion of cosmic circularity, and the deliberate Latinism of the opening line, 'si volve', suggests an instinctual 'turning' by which all beings are drawn into death's orbit. The relation of life to death, then, is not seen here as simply oppositional; being and non-being are, instead, regarded as reciprocally involved with each other. Leopardi has been said to be a poet of dualisms (Spitzer, 1963, 123), though it is perhaps more accurate to think of the relation as chiastic rather than as simply binary. This rhetorical figure of reversal (ABBA) appears frequently in the *Canti*, allowing things compared or associated to be grasped not as the same but as mutually implicated or involved, implying in a kind of deconstructive move that something can be understood for what it is only by reckoning with the existence of its other. Chiastic thinking of this sort is arguably most richly developed in the 'Chorus' where any conventional notion of the afterlife is undermined by the reversibility of the poem's main terms. As the last line tells us, the living and the dead are equally denied happiness by fate, thus suggesting that 'the common ways of the living will differ little from those of the dead' (Leopardi, 1982, 45). Life and death are interwoven with each other; indeed, we might say that they 'rhyme' with each other while remaining distinct, just as in the poem's final lines 'beato' ('happy') rhymes with the 'fate' ('fato') which makes it unrealisable. The lesson, that we cannot think of these terms in separation, is made visible in the symmetries of the poem's construction, with its central section on living (lines 14–20, from

"Vivemmo' to 'Il rimembrar'), flanked by two sections of equal measure (lines 1–13 and lines 20–32, each comprising nine septenaries and four hendecasyllabics; De Robertis, 1986, 306) and this arrangement is reinforced by the local effects of syntactical shape:

> Cosa arcana e stupenda
> Oggi è la vita al pensier nostro, e tale
> Qual de' vivi al pensiero   25
> L'ignota morte appar. Come da morte
> Vivendo rifuggia, così rifugge
> Dalla fiamma vitale
> Nostra ignuda natura;
> Lieta no ma sicura;   30
> Però ch'esser beato
> Nega ai mortali e nega a' morti il fato.

As life now seems incomprehensible ('ignota') to the dead, so death, the great unknown, is incomprehensible to the living. The chiastic reversal connecting 'la vita al pensier nostro' ('life to our thought') and 'al pensiero / L'ignota morte appar' ('to our thought death seems unknown') is then duplicated in the mirroring of 'da morte vivendo rifuggia' in 'così rifugge / Dalla fiamma vitale' (just as 'the living shrink from death', so the 'naked nature' of the dead 'shuns the vital flame'). The series is completed by the repetition of the two earlier lines 'Nostra ignuda natura / Lieta no ma sicura' (omitting the comma this time) and echoed for good measure in fate's emphatic denial ('nega [...] nega') of happiness to both the living and the dead. In this sequence of 'turning' figures, Leopardi's 'Chorus of the Dead' abandons the constraints of non-contradiction, demonstrating that a thing can indeed 'both be and not be' (Z4099). This is not to say, however, that the poem proposes 'contradiction' as some sort of alternative logic; rather, in the 'Dialogue', as we have seen, key questions are left unanswered, and the Chorus amply shows that the dead have little memory of life and are as confused about it as the nursing infant in its 'feverish dream' ('sudato sogno', line 16). 'What were we?' they ask, 'Che fu quel punto acerbo / Che di vita ebbe nome? ('What was that unripe / Moment with the name / Of life?'). Henry Weinfield's translation of 'acerbo' as 'unripe' carries more irony than the usually chosen 'bitter', given conventional associations of life with growth and maturity. To see life *sub specie aeternitatis* as merely a 'moment' is surprising, perhaps, given the way misery might seem to prolong it, but the idea that lives lived are always incomplete or unfulfilled is even more troubling.

The real irony here is dark indeed, for usual assumptions about death as something to be anticipated in the future ignore its immanent presence, inhabiting everything we see around us. Leopardi and Beckett both relish the old dictum that it is 'best not to be born, but to die quickly' (Nixon, 2011, 40), and both develop the life–death chiasmus to equate the moment of birth with that of dying (Beckett's 'womb-tomb' in *Echo's Bones*). In his poem to the Jesuit scholar Angelo Mai, Leopardi rhymes 'culla' ('cradle') with 'nulla' ('nothingness') and gives the latter almost physical presence through personification ('immote siede', it *sits,* motionless, on the grave). Beckett does something similar in *Waiting for Godot*, where Pozzo rages that 'They give birth astride of a grave, the light gleams an instant, then it's night once more' (Beckett, 2006, 83). As Cesare Galimberti has brilliantly shown (1986, 52–3), Leopardi conceives 'il nulla' ('nothingness') not as simple void or absence but (along with cognates like boredom, unhappiness and dissatisfaction) as an active constituent of the material world, circulating within in it like air around objects (see Leopardi, 1982, 177). In 'To Angelo Mai', Leopardi imagines that, for Tasso, 'Ombra reale e salda / Ti parve il nulla' ('Nothingness seemed real / A solid shape to you', lines 130–2), and Galimberti suggests that, for Leopardi too, '"Nothingness" assumes a sensible consistency, [it is] a "bodily" ["corpulenta"] figure as Vico would have called it, and dominates the sepulchral scene with the other personifications, of "idleness" and "worry"' (Galimberti, 1986, 46–7). It is this paradoxical 'presence' of nothingness that Leopardi recalls in the *Zibaldone*: 'I was frightened to find myself in the midst of nothingness, a nothing myself. I felt as if I were suffocating, thinking and feeling that all is nothing, solid nothing' ['solido nulla'] (Z85). Galimberti discerns this force of negation as something at times 'bodily' and at others just hinted at ('allusa'), and he shows it working at the very heart of the poet's literary style, 'within the sentences and the words, just as it is immanent within things' (Galimberti, 1986, 142). Linguistic negation is a consistent feature of Leopardi's verse and prose throughout his career, and he shows a particular fondness for adjectives and verbs with a negative prefix (*in-*, *s-*, *di(s)-*) which seems to cancel or erase the meaning of the word even as we read it. The figure of litotes is also much in evidence (especially in the *Operette*), with negative affirmation similarly put to work to diminish or lessen its object, and Leopardi, like Beckett, has 'a strong weakness for oxymoron' (Beckett, 1970, 33), so there are many instances of opposites forcibly cohabiting: 'felici errori' ('happy illusions') and 'vane amenità' ('empty pleasures') ('To Angelo Mai', lines 110, 114), for example, not to mention the 'ombra reale e salda' already quoted. As D. S. Carne-Ross puts it, in Leopardi's poems 'a series of negatives leads to a region or condition beyond negation, a pure, perhaps blessed, void. What is not, at this intensity, dissolves into what is. Nothingness reveals itself as the other face of being' (Carne-Ross, 1979, 188–9). One may be wary of a word such as 'blessed' in this context, though we have already seen Beckett using it in *The Unnamable* (Beckett, 1994, 36), and Malone talks, in *Malone Dies*, with great fondness of the 'blessedness of absence' (223). Perhaps this is not so surprising given that he, like Leopardi, finds that 'the only way one can speak of nothing is to speak of it as though it were something' (Beckett, 1976, 74). Once again, terms that are usually regarded as antithetical have become interchangeable, as 'nothing had happened [...] and it continued to happen' (73). Sentences like this in which literal and figurative are confusingly intertwined demonstrate Beckett's fondness for rhetorical figures of 'reversibility' (Van Hulle, 2009, 179–92), especially for chiasmus and oxymoron which produce a notable 'suspension' of sense. We should read his texts, then, as expressions not merely of pessimism but rather of Carne-Ross's 'condition beyond negation', a condition that may unexpectedly reveal something to clutch at or even, perhaps, something to celebrate. In Part II, as we shift our focus from Leopardi to Beckett, we shall attempt to map that contradictory ground or 'region' which seems to promise what Theodor Adorno remembered Beckett defining as 'a kind of positivity that is contained within pure negativity' (qtd in Weller, 2009, 229).

Part II Beckett/Leopardi
4 That Narrow Region: *First Love*

A region or a condition beyond negation: this is a region that lies at the heart of both Beckett's and Leopardi's work, and that determines the ways in which both writers understand the relation between pessimism and persistence. To move from Part I to Part II, and to switch our focus from Leopardi to Beckett, is to approach this region again, not as it reaches forwards from Leopardi to Beckett but as it stretches back from Beckett to Leopardi. It is to stage a meeting between the two writers, in which the sceptical poetics we have mapped in Leopardi's work are echoed and amplified in Beckett's.

As we have remarked, the concept of the 'region' is important to Beckett, and recurs throughout his writings. This is a word that he relishes, perhaps for the irony of its administrative aridity. The word carries something from its Latin root both of land management and of colonial rule, while allowing such fantasies of geopolitical measure to tumble into the unmapped zones of Beckett's prose. It appears as a province, with perhaps a trace of the French canton, while offering itself, too, as a region of narration, the exposed ground of literary and philosophical being. Molloy refers to this region when he talks of a voice that speaks to him, that says 'Molloy, your region is vast, you have never left it and you never shall' (Beckett, 1994, 65). This is the ground of Beckett's writing; it is also, as we shall argue throughout the second part of this Element, the ground that opens up between Beckett and Leopardi, the distinctive tract that they share, and that we are seeking here to uncover. Beckett's work is held together by the repeated scenario in which one narrative agent meets another, across a land that separates and joins them. Molloy looks across this region – what the narrator calls 'the Molloy country' – towards Moran. The narrator of *How It Is* crawls doggedly towards Pim. The narrator of *Company* looks towards a version of himself lying on his back in the dark. And throughout Beckett's drama, from Vladimir and Estragon to Hamm and Clov to Reader and Listener in *Ohio Impromptu*, this primal scene reasserts itself.

Such a meeting of narrative agents across contested ground assumes an early and provisional form in Beckett's *Watt*, a novel organised around a discussion between the protagonist Watt and the narrator Sam, who makes his appearance partway through the novel. The two meet in strange, discomposed spaces – a narrow strip between the two fences that mark off their respective 'pavilions', or a flimsy bridge across which they crawl towards each other. As they do so, they lay the groundwork for the meetings that recur over the subsequent prose and drama, the meetings in which voice passes across distance, and in which agents at a remove from one another search for a common ground that they might share. To hear a conversation passing between Beckett and Leopardi, we will argue here, is to attend to the mechanics of this meeting, which summons a kind of congress from its negation, and from the collapse of all forms of community into the non-being that underlies them.

To approach this shared ground, we might turn to the multiple forms of association between Beckett and Leopardi that glimmer in Beckett's 1945 work *Premier amour*, translated by Beckett into English as *First Love*. The title of Beckett's novella – written at a time when Leopardi was much in his mind, shortly after those nested references to the Italian poet in *Watt* – is surely a knowing reference to two of Leopardi's compositions, Leopardi's poem 'Il primo amore' and his autobiographical fragment, written in 1817 when Leopardi was only nineteen, *Memories of First Love*.

There are many associations between these various first loves that go well beyond the title that they share. In all three texts, the memories of first love, recounted by alienated and hostile young men, are characterised by a particular kind of disdain for the female object of that love, and a particular understanding of the way that loving discomposes the relation of the lover to himself (the self-estrangement that we discussed in relation to Leopardi's 'To Himself'). This experience of love is quite distinct from the other obsessive accounts of the agonies of loving with which Beckett's might be associated, in Proust or in Thomas Mann. There is a particular force in Beckett's and Leopardi's anatomisation of their first loves that binds them to each other – and to a kind of thinking that they develop across the range of their writing. For both, love is a kind of sickness that is visited upon the lover for no easily comprehensible reason, that has little or no apparent basis in a feeling of tenderness or fondness for the loved person, and whose duration is measured, from the outset, by the struggle of the lover to recover from the symptoms of that love, to return to an accommodation with self that the experience of love has disturbed.

Leopardi's poem and autobiographical fragment both turn around the moment when, as a teenage boy, he 'first knew / the strife of love' (line 2). 'Last Thursday evening', Leopardi writes in the prose fragment, 'a lady from Pesaro, a most distant relative, came to our house' (Leopardi, 1988, 1171). The 'Lady', as he says in the poem, had 'opened up a way into my heart' (Leopardi, 1987, 43). But this first experience of love affords Leopardi a close encounter not with another person but with the pain of loss from which love seems to him indistinguishable. In both the poem and the autobiographical fragment, falling in love with the Lady coincides with her leaving, in a carriage that the poet can hear from his bedroom window, as 'The horses (they would soon leave me forlorn) / Outside my parents' house stamped on the ground' (lines 41–2). 'No sooner', Leopardi writes,

> did I feel myself the prey
> Of love's fierce blazes than the little wind
> That had allayed them blew off on its way. (lines 37–9)

'I see clearly', Leopardi writes in the fragment, 'that love must be a very bitter thing', and we may hear an echo of Geulincx's annotation to his *Ethics*, where he writes, in a passage that Beckett marked in his own copy, that 'desire is nothing other than love of something absent; and it therefore contains in itself both tenderness (love), and affliction or bitterness (the anguish caused by the absence of the thing loved)' (Geulincx, 2006, 169, 314). But Leopardi's response to such bitterness is not exactly or exclusively regretful, as it allows him a form of self-examination that arises from the estrangement to which love subjects him – an estrangement with which the 'Lady' herself, the object of this love, has astonishingly little to do. 'How could I change so much from what I'd been?' (line 79), the poet wonders, finding in this alienation a pain that he 'cherishes', as it allows him to explore, in his writing, some dimension of self that love has made available to him. The fragment, and then the poem that refigures the fragment as verse, allows him to 'explore in detail the depths of love, and to be able to retrace later on exactly how this domineering passion first made its way into my heart' (Leopardi, 1988, 1175).

Beckett's *First Love* recreates the elements of Leopardi's. In Beckett's novella, the protagonist's love of a woman who goes by the name first of Lulu and then of Anna is, like Leopardi's, a cause not of happiness or tenderness but of bitterness. Lulu sits next to him on a park bench on consecutive evenings, where she sings, 'beneath her breath, as to herself and without the words fortunately, some old folk songs' (Beckett, 1995, 30). The singing disturbs him, he says – Lulu disturbs him – and so he leaves the bench, removing to an 'abandoned cowshed'; but it is here, away from Lulu, that he finds that he, like Leopardi's embittered lover, has become consumed by the flame of love. Leopardi writes in his fragment that he thinks obsessively of the Lady from Pesaro ('Yesterday morning I woke up and thought about the usual object of my love'; Leopardi, 1988, 1181). Beckett's protagonist finds too that, exiled to his cowshed, 'my thoughts were all of Lulu' (Beckett, 1995, 34). He finds himself, he says, 'inscribing the letters of Lulu in an old heifer pat', and is forced to acknowledge, in a manner that blends Leopardi's agony with Beckett's own form of comedy, that 'I had to contend with a feeling which gradually assumed, to my dismay, the dread name of love' (33). The experience, for Beckett's protagonist as for Leopardi's poet, is one which leads to a particular kind of alienation from self. 'What goes by the name of love', Beckett's narrator writes, 'is banishment' (31), and so, for Beckett and for Leopardi, to love is both to experience a strange distance from self and to seek a means of curing oneself from such love, of finding the 'little breeze / That could relieve it'. For Leopardi, even if the experience of love might open some kind of permanent void in his being, the actual love itself, of the lady from Pesaro, is fleeting. 'I am quite certain', he writes, 'that time will quickly cure me of this current love' (Leopardi, 1988, 1174). For Beckett's lover, similarly, the pain of love is transitory, and can be resolved, he finds, simply by being in the company of Lulu, or of Anna. He moves into her flat, and finds that 'Yes, already I felt better'. 'Already my love was waning, that was all that mattered' (Beckett, 1995, 41).

These elements, in Beckett's and Leopardi's first loves, echo one another. In their childishness, their disdain for the women that they 'love', their (comic) narcissism, they are both irksome, and in Beckett's case offensive ('I considered kicking her in the cunt', Beckett's narrator writes of Lulu; 31). This is the strand of mean and repellent misanthropy that runs through Beckett's earlier novel *Dream of Fair to Middling Women*, where it is also tuned to a Leopardian wavelength, a mode of mannered acerbic masculinity (counting the beads of Leopardian spleen) that has very little to redeem it. The pun in Beckett's title, playing on Tennyson's *Dream of Fair Women*, sets the misogynistic tone. But if these echoed elements sustain a kind of narrow and tedious toxicity, they also touch on other forms of literary thinking that both writers share, that are central to the more mature features of their work and that come into a particular kind of focus or thinkability precisely in their *being* shared, in the dialogue that one can hear developing between them. Indeed, it is in the anatomising of dialogue that Beckett's *First Love* looks past its stylised pessimism towards the region that his work is devoted to staking out, the narrow region that we are concerned with here and whose elements Beckett composes partly through his affinity with Leopardi. What draws Beckett's protagonist to Lulu is her voice, as she sings her disjointed snatches of old folk songs: 'The voice, though out of tune, was not unpleasant. It breathed of a soul too soon wearied ever to conclude, that perhaps least arse-aching soul of all' (30).

When the narrator leaves Lulu and their bench for the abandoned cowshed and the crusty heifer pat, it is this song that draws him back to her. He returns to the bench to find Lulu, to ask her to sing for him, and 'after a moment she began to sing and sang for some time, all the time the same song it seemed to me, without change of attitude' (37). It is in listening to this song, in testing the way that her voice carries over the ground that lies between the protagonist and Lulu, that the narrative opens onto a region composed at once of the protagonist's reluctant love and of the form of alienation, of banishment, that it inspires. 'Then I started to go', the narrator writes, as Lulu begins her song,

> And as I went I heard her singing another song, or perhaps more verses of the same, fainter and fainter the further I went, then no more, either because she had come to an end or because I had gone too far to hear her [...]. So I retraced my steps a little and stopped. At first I heard nothing, then the voice again, but only just so faintly did it carry. First I didn't hear it, then I did, I must therefore have begun hearing it, at a certain point, but no, there was no beginning, the sound emerged so softly from the silence and so resembled it. When the voice ceased at last I approached a little nearer, to make sure it had really ceased and not merely been lowered. Then in despair, saying, No knowing, no knowing, short of being beside her, bent over her, I turned on my heel and went, for good, full of doubt. (37)

Is the faintness of Lulu's voice, faintening to nothing, a consequence of the protagonist's distance from her or of her singing more quietly, and then more quietly still, until she is singing no more? This question, the protagonist soon realises, cannot be solved without his being in Lulu's presence, leaning over her with his ear against her mouth; and so he returns to her, in order to free himself of the torment of her distance from him. 'I did not feel easy when I was with her', he says, 'but at least free to think of something else than her, of the old trusty things, and so little by little, as down steps towards a deep, of nothing'

(39). As Daniel Katz has argued, the narrator's 'way of loving' is 'engaged in a dialectic with physical distance' (Katz, 2003, 251); it is only proximity to Lulu that allows the narrator access to the non-being that is the condition of his own self-congress, just as, for Leopardi's novice lover, the absence of the loved one removes him from his own 'trusty things'. Thoughts of the lady from Pesaro, Leopardi writes, 'had so completely mastered me and taken over my mind that there was no way they would leave me even while I slept' (Leopardi, 1988, 1173). Leopardi's lover has forfeited the right to think of anything other than his love and finds that 'I despise things that before I didn't use to despise, even studying, to which my mind is completely closed' (1174). And for Leopardi, as for Beckett, it is the sound of voice, of song, as it carries over distance that is a means of establishing and measuring this distance. In both the poem and the prose fragment concerning his first love, Leopardi returns to the sound of the horse and carriage outside his bedroom window in his father's house, as he waits for the Lady to leave. 'Hearing first the horses go by', he says, 'then the coach arrive', he sits, 'waiting to hear her voice for the last time' (1173):

> Fearful and silent, in the dark I turned
> My eyes and ears toward the balcony,
> Hoping to hear her voice for whom I yearned,
>
> If words should issue from her lips as she
> Was leaving, hoping for her voice alone,
> Since heaven was taking all things else away. (lines 43–8)

Voice, song, travelling over distance, forces both writers into a recognition of the insufficiency of their own being, an experience that Leopardi comes back to repeatedly in his verse. We might think of the later fragment 'The Girl's Song' (1828), which reflects on a

> Young girl's song, insistent song
> wafting from a hidden room and wandering
> in the quiet streets. (Leopardi, 2010, 351)

Or his poem 'To Silvia' (1828), in which the poet remembers that

> Sometimes I left my much beloved
> Studies and the sweat-stained pages –
> On which I spent the better part
> Of my young years – to listen from
> A terrace of my father's home
> For the sound your singing made . . . . (lines 15–20)

The distant voice of the loved one, for both writers, punctures the seal of the mind, forcing each out of the darkness of solitary reflection and into the outer world. It is for this reason, perhaps, that in 'Love and Death' (1832) Leopardi sees love as a 'sibling' of death, so that 'When an amorous affect / Born in the depth of the heart is new, / At the same time within the breast / Is sensed also / The languorous desire for death' (lines 27–31). But if the loved one's song is the sound of the deathly alienation of the lover from himself, one can't fully attend to the relation between mind, song and distance in both writers without recognising that the ground that distant song makes palpable is not only a threat to the possibility of literary self-encounter but an element of it. The absence that Beckett's narrator cherishes, as he longs to walk down his steps towards the deep of nothing, is not only drowned out by the sound of Lulu's old, endless song but composed of it, in a kind of amalgam or composition that lies at the very heart of Beckett's thinking, and of Leopardi's.

Leopardi reflects on this problem, explicitly, in the *Zibaldone*, where he ponders the particular species of pleasure that is associated with distant song – a pleasure that is bound up with the beauty of verse. 'A song', Leopardi writes – in a passage that strikes strange echoes with Beckett's *First Love* – even 'the most banal', 'heard from afar, or that seems far away without being so, or that is gradually fading and becoming imperceptible is pleasurable in itself, that is for no other reason than the vague and indefinite idea it awakens' (Z1928). The becoming imperceptible of sound – the experience that drives Beckett's narrator back to Lulu's side – is, for Leopardi, not the opposite of aesthetic experience but an element of it. Any sound 'that is so distant, in appearance or in truth, that the ear and the mind all but lose it in the vastness of space' (Z1928) brings us into contact with the region that Beckett and Leopardi share. 'There is something pleasurable', Leopardi writes,

> about an echoing place, an apartment etc., when trampling feet reverberate, or a voice, etc. Because an echo is not seen, etc. And all the more so, the vaster the place and the echo are, the farther off the echo comes from, the wider it spreads. (Z1929)

The opening gap between a sound and its impression in the mind or ear is, Leopardi suggests, the province of aesthetic pleasure. 'All these images', he writes, 'in poetry, etc., are very beautiful' (Z1929). And it is this opening gap, this intervening of an imagined tract between the narrator and the world – between the protagonist and Lulu, or Anna – that is the real ground of Beckett's novella, and that is the ontological terrain to which he returns, throughout his writing. The 'insistent song' that one can hear in Leopardi and in Beckett sits at the broken threshold that is the closest either writer can come to the ground of being – the 'ignuda natura' that poetry discloses as the estranged homeland of the self.

It is because that distant sound opens onto this difficult, vanishing foundation to being that it comes back at the close of *First Love*, in the form not of Lulu's song but of the cries of the child that is perhaps the fruit of this first love. 'There was no competing with those cries', the narrator says; 'They pursued me down the stairs and out into the street':

> If I had not known there was crying in the house I might not have heard them. But knowing it I did. I was not sure where I was. I looked among the stars and constellations for the Wains, but could not find them. And yet they must have been there. My father was the first to show them to me. (45)

In a peculiarly overwhelming gathering of the elements of which this novella is made (and of which Leopardi's fragment too is composed), the narrator's capacity to orient himself in the imagined world by the astronomy given him by his father is woven onto the spatial economy determined by distant sound, the sound of Lulu's song, the sound of the child's cries. In a powerful echo of the opening of Leopardi's 'The Recollections' (1829), in which memory is bound up with the 'Lovely constellation of the Plough' seen 'Glittering above my father's garden' (Leopardi, 2008, 135), the cries bring together astronomy, love for the father and love for the child, in one amalgamated Beckettian-Leopardian complex. 'I began playing with the cries', Beckett writes, 'a little in the same way as I had played with the song, on, back, on, back, if that may be called playing' (Beckett, 1995, 45). The cries stake out the ground of love, as they stake out the ground of literary being. As Leopardi's lover in 'First Love' finds that loving opens a permanent void in his being – 'Love is alive and still a living fire. / The lovely image breathes within my thought' (lines 100–1) – so the cries in Beckett's *First Love* persist, freeing themselves from their origin, in Lulu, or Anna, or the child, to become a feature of imagined being itself. 'For years I thought they would cease', the narrator writes; 'Now I don't think so any more. I could have done with other loves perhaps. But there it is, either you love or you don't' (45).

5 A Spectacle of Nothingness: Beckett's Trilogy

In both Beckett's and Leopardi's first loves, the 'becoming imperceptible' of sound is fashioned into a foundation of being, a foundation, in each case, that owes its persistence to its continual termination, what Moran calls, after Kant, its 'finality without end' (Beckett, 1994, 112). The conjunction of exhaustion with persistence that we uncovered, in the first part of this Element, as the shared ground of Leopardi's and Beckett's scepticism, is here given a fictional form, one which resonates richly with the 'becoming imperceptible' theorised by Deleuze and Guattari in *A Thousand Plateaus*.⁹ It is in Beckett's prose works of the forties and early fifties, from *Watt*, through the novellas (*First Love*, but also *The Calmative*, *The Expelled* and *The End*) to the novels of the trilogy, *Molloy*, *Malone Dies*, *The Unnamable*, that the Beckettian-Leopardian region we have staked out in *First Love* becomes increasingly palpable, forming a kind of mythos that is integral to the way that Beckett's fiction thinks.

In all of these works, the schema that we sketched at the opening of Section 4 repeats itself, whereby a narrating agent looks towards its narrated self, across the region we have been characterising here, the ground made of a kind of disappearance or imperceptibility. Beckett's middle prose turns around this repeated staging of an encounter with an estranged self; and in each case, with each meeting, the region across which narrator and narrated regard each other partakes of the peculiar amalgam of living and dying that Beckett finds in Leopardi. As the narrator tells us, repeatedly, in *Watt*, to touch on this region is to touch on a kind of nothingness, the kind of not-being that the narrator of *First Love* cherishes as he imagines walking down stairs into the 'deep of nothing'.¹⁰ When Watt finds himself in Mr Knott's house – when he enters with no apparent intention or volition into Mr Knott's employment as one of a series of servants who have served Mr Knott in endless succession – he 'finds himself at last', as his predecessor Arsene tells him on his arrival, 'in a situation where to do nothing exclusively would be an act of the highest value and significance' (Beckett, 1976, 39). His task, as servant to Mr Knott, is not only to *do* nothing but to be a witness to nothingness, to allow his attachment to the world to come undone, so language no longer refers to a common reality but only to this experience of non-being, that Beckett's narrators, from Belacqua onwards, so cherish. The influence of Mr Knott tends to tear words away from things, to open a gulf between words and what words signify, so the 'state in which Watt found himself', when he enters Mr Knott's employ, is one which 'resisted formulation in a way no state had ever done' (78). 'Looking at a pot', the narrator says in one of the more famous passages in the novel,

> or thinking of a pot, of one of Mr. Knott's pots, it was in vain that Watt said Pot, pot. Well, perhaps not quite in vain, but very nearly. For it was not a pot, the more he looked, the more he reflected, the more he felt sure of that, that it was not a pot at all. It resembled a pot, it was almost a pot, but it was not a pot of which one could say, Pot, pot, and be comforted. (78)

---

⁹ For 'becoming imperceptible', see Deleuze and Guattari (1987, 232–309). For the application of this theoretical apparatus to Beckett's work, see Deleuze (1997, 152–74).

¹⁰ For a range of critical and theoretical responses to Beckett's encounter with nothingness, see Caselli (2010).

To cross the threshold of Mr Knott's house is to enter into this space where the relation between names and things is broken or abstracted, and one is forced to confront a kind of nothingness at the heart of being, what we encountered in Part I as Leopardi's 'solido nulla' (Z85). This is the nothingness, too, that Watt encounters in one of the other more famous passages in the novel, in which the Galls, father and son, visit Mr Knott's house, in order to tune the piano. Watt answers a knock at the door to find standing at the threshold, 'arm in arm, an old man and a middle aged man'. The younger man, Watt recalls, declares that 'We are the Galls, father and son, and we are come what is more, all the way from town, to choon the piano' (Beckett, 1976, 67). What follows is an unexceptional scene – the younger Gall tunes the demolished piano to the best of his ability under the direction of his blind father; Watt brings refreshments on a tray; the Galls leave, having delivered the verdict that the 'strings are in flitters' and 'the piano is doomed' (69). But, just as a pot will not consent to remain a pot under the disintegrating influence of Mr Knott, so the incident of the Galls 'very soon ceased to signify for Watt a piano tuned, an obscure family and professional relation, an exchange of judgements more or less intelligible', and became instead what Watt calls a 'mere example of light commenting bodies, and stillness motion, and silence sound, and comment comment' (69–70). There is, he says, a 'fragility' to the 'outer meaning' of the incident, by virtue of which its elements tend to break down into what he calls an 'unintelligible succession of changes', that swirl around a nothingness at their heart, a nothingness which is entirely indifferent to the circumstance of 'the Galls and the piano' (70). What Watt has to confront – 'what distressed Watt' in this incident of the Galls – 'was not so much that he did not know what had happened, for he did not care what had happened, as that nothing had happened, with the utmost formal distinctness' (73), that 'nothing had happened, with all the clarity and solidity of something' (73). To be in the negative presence of Mr Knott is to experience this Leopardian 'solid nothing', so that 'Watt learned toward the end of his stay in Mr Knott's house to accept that nothing had happened, that a nothing had happened, learned to bear it and even, in a shy way, to like it' (77).

Nothingness here becomes a kind of substance that is the material ground of Beckett's imagination – the ground that Molloy refers to, throughout *Molloy*, as his 'region', the region across which Molloy struggles towards his mother, and the region across which Moran travels with his son, in his bid to track Molloy down. In *Molloy*, this space appears in part as a landscape that has become recognisable as it is repeated across Beckett's writing, a landscape, Molloy says, that is 'characteristic of my region' (Beckett, 1994, 65). As Molloy drags himself with his crutches through the forest towards his mother at the close of the first part of *Molloy*, he is heading towards the place from which the very possibility of narration emerges – the space of his mother's room, in which Molloy himself sits down to write his narrative. Through his long months of crawling in the woods, Molloy despairs of ever finding his way out, of ever seeing again the city of his birth. But, eventually, 'the day came when the forest ended and I saw the light, the light of the plain, exactly as I had foreseen' (90). The liberation from the forest, though, leads only to another kind of immobility, as Molloy finds himself stuck in a ditch. 'The forest ended', Molloy writes, 'in a ditch, I don't know why, and it was in this ditch that I became aware of what had happened to me' (90). This ditch might carry an echo from the passage in Leopardi's *Zibaldone* that we quoted earlier, where Leopardi offers an epigrammatic picture of 'life' as the 'journey of a crippled and sick man' which ends 'at a precipice or ditch, in which inevitably he falls' (Z4162–3). It recalls, too, Leopardi's 'Night Song of a Wandering Shepherd in Asia' where a 'Little old white-haired man' struggles 'up mountain and down valley, / over sharp rocks, across deep sands and bracken, / through wind and storm', only to arrive at a 'terrible, immense abyss / into which he falls, forgetting everything' (Leopardi, 2010, 195).

Molloy's journey through wild, rugged, arduous places ends up in Leopardi's ditch (in which 'life' is really only the inevitability of death); and it is from here that Molloy looks towards his mother and towards the scene of his own narrative invention – the invention of himself. 'I looked at the plain rolling away as far as the eye could see', Molloy says; 'I saw, faintly outlined against the horizon, the towers and steeples of a town' (Beckett, 1994, 90). To cross this plain is to effect the conjoining of narrator and narrated, of living and dead self, to find in writing an overcoming of nothingness, in which, in Leopardi's terms, 'the soul receives life' from its encounter with 'the perpetual death of things' (Z261). But for Beckett, as for Leopardi, this region is one that cannot be crossed, or whose crossing is also an uncrossing. 'I could not assume', Molloy thinks, that the town he looks on was his. 'It is true', he says, that 'the plain seemed familiar, but in my region all the plains looked alike' (Beckett, 1994, 90–1). And in any case, he goes on, the question of whether the town he looks upon is his own town is academic. 'Whether it was my town or not' he says,

> whether somewhere under that faint haze my mother panted on, or whether she poisoned the air a hundred miles away, were ludicrously idle questions for a man in my position, though of undeniable interest on the plane of pure knowledge. For how could I drag myself over that vast moor, where my crutches would fumble in vain. (91)

Molloy ends, in a sense, here, at the threshold between the first section of the novel and the second, between Molloy's narrative and Moran's. As Molloy looks across the impassable plain towards the place in which he gives himself his literary birth, Beckett's novel brings the possibility of narration into a terrible identity with its impossibility, the impossibility of ever freeing life from the death that underwrites it. Molloy cannot cross that gulf that separates him from himself, and so the ground itself becomes a form of nothingness, an unnarratability that is woven into narration itself. This is the Leopardian region composed of the chiastic identity of statement and denial, something and nothing, that we traced, through Galimberti, in the first part of this Element. And it is this ground too that stretches between Moran and Molloy, between the first part of *Molloy* and the second. Moran finds that he can, after a fashion, cross the divide between the two sections of the novel. He is able to consort with Molloy, but he can only do so in his mind, in some imaginary space, 'far from the world, its clamours, frenzies, bitterness and dingy light' (111). Safe at home, before he heads out on his quest to discover the 'real' Molloy, Moran can meet with an imaginary Molloy, one that he finds 'ready-made in my head' (112). It is only when he is 'steeped' in a world of imagined things, non-existent things, at 'the mercy of sensations which happily I know to be illusory' (111), that he can enter into Molloy's being, for 'where Molloy could not be', he says, 'nor Moran either for that matter, there Moran could bend over Molloy' (112). He can bend over him, in the dark of his bedroom, and by the light of his imagination, but when he tries to cross the region that separates them, he finds that Molloy recedes farther and farther from view, until Moran, too, is marooned in that plane, between forest and city, in which ground gives way to groundlessness, being to non-being, and the possibility of common life gives way to nothingness. Moran enters into the Molloy region only to find that Molloy eludes capture, and so he is instructed to return home, to his own scene of narration, where he writes a narrative that does not secure his being, or Molloy's, but cancels them both out. Moran's report begins, famously, with the declaration that 'It is midnight. The rain is beating on the windows' (92); it ends with Moran sitting at his desk to write his report, after his failed search for Molloy. 'I went back into the house and wrote, It is midnight. The rain is beating on the windows. It was not midnight. It was not raining' (176).

To approach the region that Beckett and Leopardi share – to understand the commingling within it of life and death, of being and nothingness – is to breathe the air of this space that opens between Moran and Molloy, between Molloy and himself. It is to find that narrative life is so closely bound up with the impossibility of narration that the very movement towards the affirmation of being becomes a kind of negation, as the narrator of *The Unnamable* finds that he can 'proceed' only by 'aporia', by 'affirmations and negations invalidated as uttered' (293). But it is also to find that aesthetic beauty – so skirted about, in both writers, with sceptical disavowals – makes of the failure of narration a kind of joy that survives that scepticism, that *thrives* on it. At a critical moment in *Molloy*, as Moran reaches the end of his search, and his 'colleague' Gaber visits him, to instruct him to return home, the joy of beauty makes an odd kind of appearance, in the form of a quotation from Keats's *Endymion*.[11] As Jean-Michel Rabaté has noted, it is here, at the failed end of Moran's quest, that he is 'suddenly seized by a Kantian sense of the beauty of the world' (Rabaté, 2016, 95). Moran asks Gaber if their boss, Youdi, is angry with him, for failing to find Molloy. 'Angry', Gaber says, 'don't make me laugh. He keeps rubbing his hands from morning to night', and 'chuckling to himself'. He is not angry, and in fact, Gaber says, Youdi gave him a message, as he chuckled and rubbed his hands together, a gift of sorts to pass on to Moran, as payment for his labours. 'What did he tell you?', Moran says, desperate for this piece of wisdom, this word from the horse's mouth:

> He said to me, said Gaber, Gaber, he said –. Louder! I cried. He said to me, said Gaber, Gaber, he said, life is a thing of beauty, Gaber, and a joy for ever. He brought his face nearer mine. A joy for ever, he said, a thing of beauty, Moran, and a joy for ever. (Beckett, 1994, 165)

At this point in the novel, as Moran has been divested of his humanity and become a crawling beast of the field, as derelict as Molloy himself, this message from Youdi seems cruel, sinister, a bad joke. 'A thing of beauty is a joy for ever', Keats writes at the opening of *Endymion*. 'Its loveliness increases; it will never / Pass into nothingness' (Keats, 1982, 65). But here, the possibility of aesthetic beauty has passed, precisely, into nothingness, the nothingness that lies at the heart of Molloy's narrow region. Beauty passes into nothingness, as Moran intuits early in his report, as he sits amid his bourgeois comfort and marvels at the spectacle of the sun setting over his wooded garden. 'A great joy', he says, 'surged over me at the sight of so much beauty, so much promise. I turned away with a sigh, for the joy inspired by beauty is often not unmixed' (Beckett, 1994, 117).

It is this admixture, perhaps, that leads Youdi to rub his hands, to gloat like a vindictive god over the failures of beauty to conquer nothingness; but at the heart of *Molloy*, at the very foundation of Beckett's middle works, is a formulation of the relation between beauty and nothingness that has a Leopardian rather than a Keatsian character – a relation that is approached,

---

[11] For a recent account of Beckett's relationship with Keats, which also touches on his debt to Leopardi, see Keanie (2024).

in *Molloy* as in *First Love*, through the experience of sound, of voice, music, song, as it crosses the aesthetic terrain. Any sound is beautiful, Leopardi writes in a passage we have already quoted, that is 'so distant, in appearance or in truth, that the ear and the mind all but lose it in the vastness of space' (Z1928). The becoming imperceptible of sound, in Leopardi's and Beckett's first loves, opens onto a nothingness which is also a beauty and a joy – not the threat to be overcome but the ground in which life and death are amalgamated. And at the heart of *Molloy*, Beckett has stretched out a particular kind of hearing apparatus, one that is attuned to precisely that moment, in *First Love*, when sound sits on the threshold between the perceptible and the imperceptible, and where voice passes across the region that the novel makes available to thought, and across the threshold that separates the first part from the second. As Molloy is crawling through the forest, he diverts himself by listening out for the 'forest murmurs' (Beckett, 1994, 89). He perhaps has half in mind the sound that Leopardi's lover associates with his lady in 'Il primo amore', as her 'soft elusive movements' arouse in his soul 'a thousand confused, uncertain thoughts', 'The way a forest's foliage in the fall, / From breezes riffling through it, can be stirred / To long, uncertain murmurings' (lines 31–3). Molloy strains his ears for those forest murmurs, but 'it was in vain I listened. I could hear nothing of the kind, but rather, with much good will and a little imagination, at long intervals a distant gong' (89). 'For a moment', he thinks, 'I dared hope it was only my heart, still beating' (as Leopardi's 'To Himself' is addressed to his own still beating heart); but even as Molloy looks within himself for the origin of this sound, Beckett's novel looks in another direction, not towards oneself but towards the common nothingness that underlies Beckett's and Leopardi's poetics. The gong that Molloy can hear, in place of the forest murmurs, has echoed through the pale air of his region, and has passed across the threshold between part one and part two of the novel. Molloy's gong is sounding, even as he drags himself through the forest on his crutches, in Moran's darkened bedroom, as Moran bends over Molloy. Having tracked Molloy down, having found him in that place in his head where no light could ever be, and no bodies, Moran says, 'I felt equal to facing Gaber's report'. 'It seemed', he says, 'as if the enquiry were about to start at last' – but 'it was then', at that moment of inauguration, 'that the sound of a gong, struck with violence filled the house' (116).

The common nothingness that this sound summons, as it passes across the threshold of the perceptible, is the shared terrain of Beckett's and Leopardi's thought. Across the long tract of Beckett's middle trilogy, his narrative task is to come ever closer to this Leopardian substrate to his thinking, a thin sheet of being in which a commons is summoned from its impossibility. As Molloy looks from his ditch towards the distant town, this thin sheet takes the form of an eardrum, a hearing apparatus that brings together the sonic elements of which the novel is made. 'At this painful juncture', Molloy says, as he realises that he can't cross that plain on his crutches, 'I heard a voice telling me not to fret, that help was coming. Literally. These words struck it is not too much to say [...] clearly on my ear, and on my understanding' (91). Whatever succour, whatever continued investment in beauty and joy the trilogy can muster, comes to possibility in this odd vibrating integument, this biological register of the becoming imperceptible of sound.

As the trilogy continues, as the narrative voice passes from Molloy and Moran to Malone and then to the unnamable narrator, the apparatuses of the novel form are steadily dismantled, in the same way that Moran as a 'character' is slowly discomposed as he makes his way towards Molloy. The machinery of novel imagining continually denudes itself, scraping away its own surfaces until it reaches towards a form of nothingness, the notness that we find at the heart of Mr Knott's house. But as Beckett's narrative approaches the condition of non-being, it comes closer, too, to the amalgam of life and death that he forges in part through his conversation with Leopardi. What this denuding tendency opens onto, finally, is not pure negativity but a kind of threshold. This is what Malone calls 'the threshold of being no more' (194), and what the unnamable narrator calls, in his final sentence, 'the threshold of my story, before the door that opens on my story' (418). 'They'll tell me who I am', the unnamable narrator says, nearing the frenzied pitch of his conjoining of naming with unnaming. 'They'll have said who I am, and I'll have heard, without an ear I'll have heard, and I'll have said it, without a mouth I'll have said it, I'll have said it inside me, then in the same breath outside me' (386). Hearing, speaking, survive the scraping away of the apparatuses of being, until *The Unnamable* presents us with the very thinnest of surfaces, the barest, most naked of natures, where being and non-being meet. 'Perhaps that's what I feel', the narrator says,

> perhaps that's what I am, the thing that divides the world in two, on the one side the outside, on the other the inside, that can be thin as foil, I'm neither one side nor the other, I'm in the middle, I'm the partition, I've two surfaces and no thickness, perhaps that's what I feel, myself vibrating, I'm the tympanum, on the one hand the mind, on the other the world, I don't belong to either. (386)

This is what lies at the heart of Beckett's work, the thinnest of conjunctions that brings Sam into his peculiar union with Watt, as they crawl towards each other across their flimsy bridge. A kind of vibrating sensation, Leopardi's 'spectacle of nothingness', which both writers find at the edge and the foundation of life, and which composes the very stuff of our naked nature.

6 The World Is Mud: *How It Is*

It is easy to imagine that, in the passage from Beckett's middle to his later works, the influence of Leopardi, so evident in *Dream*, and present, if occluded, in *Watt*, starts to wane. But it is our contention here that the conjunction between Leopardi's and Beckett's poetics that one can discern in the early and middle phases of Beckett's career extends throughout the later work, from *Texts for Nothing* to *Worstward Ho* and *Stirrings Still*. Across these works, the relation between Beckett and Leopardi is grounded not so much in reference or allusion as in a particular kind of affinity which does not wane but rather deepens into a shared literary and philosophical sensibility. The common elements to which we have returned, in which Beckett's thinking conjoins with Leopardi's from *Dream* to *The Unnamable*, persist throughout the works, both fiction and drama, written after the close of the trilogy, where they form a kind of substrate to Beckett's imagination – the particular mode of imagining that Beckett works so grimly and tirelessly to extend past the moment of its own death. The capacity to find a common ground between nothing and something, founded on Leopardi's discovery that 'the spectacle of nothingness is itself a thing' (Z259); the opening of a channel between life and death that both writers establish through the fashioning of a form of posthumous poetics, expressed most clearly in Leopardi's 'Chorus of the Dead'; the fascination with Leopardi's 'becoming imperceptible' of song and voice, as this touches on the vanishing terrain of literary being; and the gathering together of all of these elements in the formulation of a kind of naked nature, Leopardi's 'natura ignuda': these shared features of both writers' imaginations form the very territory that Beckett stakes out, from *Texts for Nothing* to *Stirrings Still*.

These common elements return, and, as they do so, Leopardi's influence is interwoven with those other conjoined figures who recur in Beckett's imaginative pantheon. Woven into Leopardi's presence is the influence of Dante, which has been traced so finely by Daniela Caselli; the influence of Geulincx, as illuminated by David Tucker; the influence of Proust, which Beckett himself filters through what he calls, in a passage we have already quoted, the 'wisdom of all the sages, from Brahma to Leopardi' (Beckett, 1965, 18).[12] These figures together produce an anatomy of the constrained imagination, the imagination hemmed in by what Beckett calls Leopardi's 'pessimism'. The Geulingian predicament that we have already explored – in which the freedom to invent is limited to our ability to crawl feebly against the current that propels us irresistibly towards death, so we are 'free', as Molloy puts it, 'on the black

---

[12] See Caselli (2009) and Tucker (2012). For the relation between Beckett and Proust, see Zurbrugg (1988).

boat of Ulysses, to crawl towards the East, along the deck' (Beckett, 1994, 51) – is reproduced and reinforced in these works, with a kind of brutal insistence. Leopardi's splenetic scepticism merges with Geulincx's fatalist ascetism ('Where you can do nothing there also you should desire nothing'; Geulincx, 2006, 305), and with Schopenhauerian will-lessness, to carve out the narrow tracts of Beckett's later works. Leopardi's presence can be everywhere felt in this tireless depiction of constraint. But if these works are determined in part by Leopardi's pessimism, what makes the continued dialogue between the two writers so productive, and so mutually transformative, is that it allows for a critical reappraisal of the contradiction that we traced in Part I of this Element – the contradiction between exhaustion and persistence, between fatalism and resolution, which both powers their work and leads to a kind of interpretive aporia beyond which is it very difficult for a critical reading, of either writer, to proceed.

This shared analysis of contradiction as a ground to being is perhaps nowhere more fully developed than in *How It Is*, the most extended work of prose fiction that Beckett writes after *The Unnamable*, and the most austere and forbidding exploration of the mechanics of literary invention in his – or possibly any – body of work. The text might be thought of as taking place, in its entirety, in the space of that line from 'To Himself' – 'e fango è il mondo', 'the world is mud'. It tells the story of a journey through a kind of universal mud. This journey, as it is described by the narrator, is broken into three parts. In part one, the nameless protagonist journeys through the mud alone, heading towards another inhabitant of this infernal or purgatorial place, whose name is Pim, and whom it is the task of the unnamed protagonist to torment. Part two tells of the period that the protagonist spends with Pim, as he torments him, stabbing his anus with a can opener, digging his fingernails into his armpit, to elicit from him a few human cries, and a faint voice with which he murmurs into the mud. The third and final part of the story tells of the protagonist alone once more having been abandoned by Pim, during which time he murmurs, himself, into the mud, with his own faint voice, telling the story of how it was before Pim, how it was with Pim, how it was after Pim, and finally how it is now.

Such a tale seems grim enough, an unadorned picture of Leopardi's world as mud, and 'nature', as Leopardi puts it, as the 'brute, hidden power that ordains / Our pain, the common doom'. Beckett's text is an extension of those lines in 'To Himself', or of Leopardi's *Copernicus: A Dialogue*, a fable in the *Operette morali* in which the sun decides that it can't be bothered to shine, either on the 'First Hour' of the day or on the 'Last'. The 'First Hour' says to the Sun, in Leopardi's fable, that it's time to rise and commence the day. But the Sun replies that the First Hour should 'leave me alone': 'Come what may, I'm not moving'

(Leopardi, 1982, 417). 'How can the day be', the First Hour replies, 'if your Excellency isn't kind enough to come out as usual?'. But the Sun is intractable. 'I'm tired' he says, 'of this continuous going around to give light to a few little animals that live on a handful of mud—so small that I, who have quite good eyesight, can't even see it' (417–19).

The sun refuses to shine, and so, the First Hour says, the creatures who live on that ball of mud will be deprived of light and of warmth. By what light will they find their way, he asks. 'To have to keep their lamps burning or to keep so many candles lit the whole space of the day will be excessively costly.' And how will they manage in the cold when, without the heat provided by the Sun, 'the firewood of all the forests won't be enough to keep them warm'. 'Besides which', the First Hour says,

> they'll also starve to death, for the earth will no longer bear fruit. And so in the course of a few years, even the brood of those poor animals will be lost. And when they'll have gone groping here and there about the earth for a while, looking for something to eat and to keep warm, finally, after there is nothing left to swallow and when the last spark of fire is no more, they'll all die in the dark, frozen like pieces of rock crystal. (419)

This picture, of creatures crawling through the mud of an abandoned planet, deprived of the light of reason, or the warmth of company, with certain death as the only horizon, is a striking companion piece to Beckett's tale of barely human animals crawling in the mud. The lamps that the 'First Hour' imagines might take the place of the sun's light appear in Beckett's tale, where they are used to illuminate the scene in the mud. There would need to be a 'witness', Beckett's narrator reasons, for us to see and record this subterranean existence. So he invents a figure, named Kram, or Krem, who examines the crawling creature, the nameless protagonist. 'He lives bent over me', the narrator says, 'all my visible surface bathing in the light of his lamps' (Beckett, 1996, 19). The lamps are necessary, both in Beckett's tale and in Leopardi's, because the sun is 'extinguished', as it is in Beckett's *Endgame*, so all the world is 'grey', 'light black. From pole to pole' (Beckett, 2006, 107). The narrator of *How It Is* is granted, from time to time, an image of a still or once living world, 'up above in the light', 'a fine image fine I mean in movement and colour blue and white of clouds in the wind' (Beckett, 1996, 30); but these are images of a world that has already ended. '[B]lue and white of sky', the narrator says, 'a moment still April morning in the mud it's over it's done I've had the image the scene is empty a few animals still then goes out no more blue' (34). Beckett's mud-bound creatures, like Leopardi's, need artificial light in order to see and be seen; and so too they are in need of artificial food. They make their way up and down through a dead earth that will yield no food, and so it happens that in their path they find sacks – to each crawling creature its own sack, distributed by some unseen hand – which contain tins of food, a preserved remainder or residue of life, which is the only sustenance that extends this glimmer of being past the threshold between the living and the dead, the above and the below.

Both Beckett and Leopardi present us with the proposition of a world that is mud, or perhaps a world where the 'so-called mud' is 'nothing more than all our shit', in which there are 'billions of us crawling and shitting in their shit hugging like a treasure in their arms the wherewithal to crawl and shit a little more' (58). This is a feature of their shared pessimism, their rejection of all fanciful distractions from the naked condition of being. But what is so striking about this dialogue between Beckett and Leopardi is that the nakedness that it proposes and presupposes – the absolute refusal of what Beckett calls any 'addition' to being[13] – becomes itself that very addition that it denies – an addition that arises from those elements that we have already examined here, those elements that Beckett and Leopardi share as the foundation of their literary thinking. It is the sudden leap of *How It Is* – that takes Beckett from the impasse at the end of *The Unnamable* to the later theatrical and prose works – to craft a form that can generate narrative possibility from the agonising synthesis of oppositions that brings the trilogy to a halt. *How It Is* is an extended, exquisitely painful exploration of the contradiction that the impulse towards contraction, minima, contains within it, as an automatic mathematical principle, an opposite impulse towards expansion, maxima. The chiastic tendencies that we traced in Leopardi's verse, and which fashion the very terrain of Beckett's imagination, reach here their most intense pitch. This kind of problem, this bidirectional tendency towards addition and subtraction, is evident from the first line of *How It Is*, in the tension that is established there between the multiplication and the eradication of voice: 'how it was I quote before Pim with Pim after Pim how it is three parts I say it as I hear it' (7). The text that is being offered to us here, we are told in the opening line, is a quotation – and one which only comes to an end with the final line of the text, the final mumbled paragraph: 'good good end at last of part three and last that's how it was end of quotation after Pim how it is' (160).

This text does not come from the narrator, is not owned by the narrator, but is a quotation, a text at one remove (the only words in *How It Is* that escape the gravitational pull of quotation, perhaps, are 'how it was after Pim how it is').

---

[13] The question of addition to being, and how to renounce it, is central to Beckett's late trilogy. From the repeated refrain in *Company* – 'What an addition to company that would be' (Beckett, 1992b, 22) – to the narrator's instruction to himself in *Worstward Ho*, 'Add? Never' (111) – the works can be seen as an attempt to convert addition into subtraction.

Such a device is familiar to any reader of Beckett's work, as he has employed it, at least since *Watt*, as a means of simultaneously claiming and disowning the responsibility for speech. When Sam and Watt meet across the narrow region we mapped out earlier, they do so across what might be thought of as a field of quotation, an expanding and contracting zone of mingled voices. In a repeated refrain, Sam insists that he is not responsible for his narration, that he is simply quoting a tale told to him by Watt, who is speaking from the non-space occupied by Mr Knott. 'For all that I know on the subject of Mr. Knott', Sam says, 'and of all that touched Mr. Knott, and on the subject of Watt, and of all that touched Watt, came from Watt, and from Watt alone' (Beckett, 1976, 123). Sam is quoting Watt, as the narrator of *How It Is* is quoting from some unidentified voice, similarly shrouded in nothingness. And the beauty of this device, for the narrators both of *Watt* and of *How It Is*, is that it allows the narrator to dispense with the voice, to return it to the nothingness whence it came. This is the gambit employed by the narrator in the closing pages of *How It Is*, as the narrative builds to its breathless climax: 'all this business', the narrator says, 'of voices yes quaqua yes of other worlds yes of someone in another world yes whose kind of dream I am yes said to be yes that he dreams all the time yes tells all the time' (158); 'all this business of sacks deposited yes at the end of a cord no doubt yes of an ear listening to me' (159); 'all this business of above yes light yes skies yes a little blue yes a little white yes the earth turning yes bright and less bright yes little scenes yes' (159): the whole shebang, it is 'all balls', 'all balls yes', 'only me in any case alone yes in the mud yes the dark yes' (159).

Quote a tale, borrow a voice to tell a tale, in order to eradicate that voice, and so to leave yourself in a space of non-existence, the dark, the mud of a naked nature, an 'ignuda natura' that has freed itself from being, the 'orgy of false being' that is the consequence, the narrator says, of 'life in common' (76). To live, up above in the light, is continually to lose yourself, to falsify yourself, continually to experience yourself as another, as another person, or as yourself in the past or in the future, the person to come or the person who has been, before Pim, with Pim, after Pim, how it is. To live is continually to die, to evacuate the space and time and matter of one's own being. And so you hold before you the voice that tells you the story of your own life – that gives us, as Estragon puts it, the 'impression we exist' (Beckett, 2006, 64). You hold it before you, in order to disavow it, and to return yourself to a kind of undifferentiated mud, a kind of borderline creatureliness, in which one remains identical with oneself, and one is entirely sunk in one's own naked matter. It is to commit one's body to the ground, earth to earth, dust to dust, to the 'muck where all is identical' (Beckett, 1996, 121).

But – and this is the crux of *How It Is*, the original propulsive force that drives this creature, these creatures, these billions of creatures to crawl endlessly through the mud – to eradicate voice, to return to a complete undifferentiated identity with one's own naked matter, is the work, itself, of the voice. This is why the first mover of *How It Is* is quotation. To be, in one's own naked nature, is to borrow a voice with which to eradicate the addition, the differentiation, the non-identity that is native to narrative voice, the voice whose very nature is to carry being away from oneself. The narrative agent in *How It Is* 'sets out to seek out the true home' (111), the true home as that identity with oneself that one can never achieve; and that setting out, even as it aims for reduction to oneness, involves duplication to twoness, and then threeness, and then unnumberable multiplicity, infinite increase, infinite regress. The nameless narrator, crawling through the mud, aims for part three, when he will finally be able to say 'how it is' (160). But to get there, to arrive at the experience of being, in which one is replete in oneself, requires the narrator to divide himself from himself, as the formal logic of the text requires the voice to 'divide into three a single eternity' (26). And the materialisation of this distance of self from self is Pim, the other body in the mud, the body towards which the nameless narrator crawls in part one, with whom the narrator is conjoined in part two, and who abandons the narrator in part three. Each nameless narrative agent requires its Pim, as Watt requires Sam, as the Unnamable narrator requires Molloy, Moran, Malone, Mahood, Worm. Namelessness cannot sustain itself, so it crawls through the mud that is also the ink of the text, the wet black stuff of narrative voice, towards that body, which it will torment, and which it will make speak for it, will employ as a prosthetic, so that the soundless voice sounds in the mud. As the narrator protagonist reaches the body of Pim in part two – as he plunges his can opener into Pim's anus, scratches at his armpit, and scrawls his script into the skin of Pim's back for Pim to repeat in a murmur to the mud – he is employing him, as the unnamable narrator puts it, as a 'vice-exister' (Beckett, 1994, 317), a bodily form, as Malone puts it, with which the 'unchanging' narrative agent 'seeks relief from its formlessness' (198).

The nameless narrative agent needs its surrogates, in order to declare its freedom from them, in order to borrow from them the voice with which to annihilate voice. Pim is an inanimate thing, a slab of flesh, which the voice adopts, brings to life, in order to discard. 'he would never', the narrator says,

> Pim we're talking of Pim never be but for me anything but a dumb limp lump flat for ever in the mud but I'll quicken him you wait and see and how I can efface myself behind my creature when the fit takes me. (Beckett, 1996, 58)

The narrative desire that has driven Beckett's work, from *Watt* through the novels of the trilogy, reaches here, in *How It Is*, a kind of apotheosis. The process of adopting a body with which to materialise voice, and of discarding that body in order to free oneself from the messy business of material being, is squeezed here into a single moment of simultaneous adoption and discarding. The voice that speaks here is at once the agent that effaces itself behind its creature, and the creature that lives in that agent's stead. This is the first appearance, in Beckett's work, of what he later calls the 'devised deviser devising it all for company', the devised deviser 'devising figments to temper his nothingness' (Beckett, 1992b, 37). The formal achievement of *How It Is* is that it invents, right before us, a language with which to express this chiastic unity of addition and subtraction, of solitude and company, in the condition of its unity. The radical form of the text is a kind of materialisation, a bodying forth of this unity, what Beckett calls, in a 1955 letter to David Hayman, the 'identification of contraries' (Beckett, 2011, 537). All the residua of the novel form that one finds in Beckett's preceding works are gone, so what we are left with is a wriggling protoplasm, the genetic material of the imagination, stripped of its imaginary elements. It expands to absorb the voice that it quotes and contracts to expel it, endlessly, eternally, like a perpetual motion machine, or a self-enclosed galaxy. It is a serpent that eats its own tail, a stretch of narrative duration that absorbs its moment of origin, and its moment of termination, into its own pulsing, peristaltic totality. It is a machine that creates its own fuel, in the form of those sacks containing tins of sardines or tuna – that creates its own fuel, and consumes it, and excretes it, and consumes it again. It is a narrative tract that binds part one to part three, so that the beginning and the end are part of one unbroken moment, and the tormentor is the victim, the victim is the tormentor. The 'unthinkable first' moment, like Leopardi's 'First Hour', is bound to the unthinkable last, so that 'at each instant each ceased' (Beckett, 1996, 132). The pulsing of the prose is the writhing of an 'imagination' who 'drinks that drop of piss of being and who with his last gasp pisses it to drink' (144).

Except that it is not. It does not. It is the gift of *How It Is* to fashion a form in which contraction is bound to expansion, as Beckett suggests that, for Giordano Bruno and James Joyce, 'the maxima and minima of particular contraries are one and indifferent' (Beckett, 1972, 6). But it is a part of this discovery, one that is difficult to focus or to conceive of, that this unity itself contains within it a disunity (in the dizzying, vertiginous realisation that the merging of identity and difference applies too to that merging, so that the identification of the contrary between unity and multiplicity results not only in a unity but also in a multiplicity). In Beckett, as in Leopardi, the force that brings oppositions together, that makes nothing and something identical to one another, also splits them apart, so the more intensely the narrative seeks to absorb everything there is into itself, the more intensely it encounters an imaginary element that escapes the narrative machinery, that cannot be contained with it. This is Beckett's inheritance of Leopardi's legacy – his inheritance and radicalisation of Leopardi's poetics, which brings both writers to the vanishing point of their thinking, that difficult, airless place, where termination meets with continuation, silence with sound, and despair with a kind of pale, unenchanted hope.

We can see this meeting place in *How It Is* in the recurrence of those shared elements that we have already traced in both writers' accounts of their first loves. It is the 'becoming imperceptible' (Z1928) of sound, Leopardi writes, that stakes out the vanishing point, where the voice of the other is on the brink of being lost to us, the fulcrum at which the frail junction between our being and that of our loved one is on the point of being severed. This is the same junction that Beckett's narrator marks out, in *First Love*, as he plays with Lulu's song, or with the cries of his child. Song and cry grow fainter as the narrator moves farther away from his lover and from his child, until finally they can no longer be heard, and so sound passes into silence, and 'life in common' (Beckett, 1996, 76) passes into life 'alone yes in the mud yes the dark yes' (160). And it is this very drama, this play of sound as it passes over distance, that re-emerges, in *How It Is*, as a distant echo of *Premier amour* and 'Il primo amore'. As the narrator crawls towards Pim in part two, he re-enacts the earlier protagonist's approach to the bench, in *First Love*, on which Lulu sits singing her song. He crawls to Pim, who is lying face down in the mud; he reaches his arm around his shoulders, delving down beneath the mud, to feel his mouth, to feel with his fingers the brief movement of the lower face: 'my right hand seeks his lips let us try and see this pretty movement more clearly'; 'the hand approaches under the mud', and 'it's as I thought he's singing'. As the narrator reaches Pim, he finds that he has a voice, and that he is singing: 'I can't make out the words the mud muffles or perhaps a foreign tongue perhaps he's singing a lied in the original' (63). He is singing, and the narrator finds that there is 'a human voice there within an inch or two my dream perhaps even a human mind if I have to learn Italian obviously it will be less amusing' (63).

When the narrator hears Pim's song, and then later when he hears his cries, what kind of distance does that sound traverse? This is the central question of *How It Is*. The nameless narrator crawls towards Pim, he scrawls a script on his back, the script we are reading. Pim gives that script a voice, murmuring the tale into the mud, as he lives in the narrator's stead. 'I let him know', the narrator says, 'that I too Pim my name Pim there he has more difficulty a moment of confusion irritation it's understandable' (66). When the narrator reaches Pim, he does not only encounter another, another person to love and to torment; he also encounters himself, as the voice that Pim speaks with is the voice that the narrator is quoting, the voice that was 'once without quaqua on all sides then in me when the panting stops' (7). The nameless narrator adopts the name of his surrogate, and so, when he hears his song, when the sound reaches him through the mud, he is only hearing the song that is playing in his own head, 'the same air it seems to me', the song that has been playing inside the echo chamber of Beckett's work since the narrator of *First Love* heard Lulu singing on her bench. When he listens to Pim's song, when he 'lends his ear to our murmur', he 'does no more than lend it to a story of his own devising' (151). To listen to Pim, he says, catching a faint echo of the title of Leopardi's poem, is to 'listen to himself' (151), as the text makes of these different people, speaker and hearer, tormentor and victim, narrator and protagonist, one seamless being. The narrator asks Pim, as he finds him in the mud, in part two, if it might be possible that 'Pim loved me a little' if 'I loved him a little in the dark the mud in spite of all a little affection find someone at last someone find you at last live together' (82). This is the question, too, that the narrator asks himself in *First Love*. What kind of distance is there between the narrator and Lulu? The narrator and Pim? The urge to cross that distance, to absorb the loved one into the closed circle of the self – the attempt to restore the unity of the ego that is the subject of both *First Love* and 'Il primo amore' – is frustrated in all three texts (*First Love*, 'Il primo amore', *How It Is*) by its very intensity. As the narrator reaches Pim, and drapes his body over him in the mud, the two are 'glued together' (82). Pim's mouth is pressed against the narrator's ear – 'a mouth an ear sly old pair glued together' (87). The becoming one of two is not a becoming, if one and two are somehow the same, if the distance between mouth and ear is eradicated, so completely that it is as if it had never been.

One cannot love under the circumstances. How can one love this other, if the desire to love them means that one makes of them a version of oneself? How can one love if, as the female protagonist of Beckett's harrowing play *Rockaby* finds, the yearning for an 'other living soul' leads her to become 'her own other', her 'own other living soul' (Beckett, 2006, 441)? The formal logic of *How It Is*, as well as its driving desire, leads to this collapse of the distinction between self and other, narrator and Pim, mouth and ear, so the eardrum, the tympan that is the final threshold of *The Unnamable*, becomes not a boundary between one person and another but a kind of epidermal sack, or caul, which encloses this narrative being within itself, within its own precincts. With 'my right shoulder overriding his', the narrator says, 'my head its face in the mud and his its right cheek in the mud his mouth against my ear our hairs tangled together', he has the 'impression that to separate us one would have to sever them' (Beckett, 1996, 100), one would have to sever mouth from ear, as these conjoined bodies in the mud – Pim's and the narrator's, but also the billions of bodies, in the mud and the shit, as they extend backwards and forwards infinitely in both directions, victims and tormentors, speakers and hearers – become all one body. The 'coming into contact of mouth and ear', the narrator says, 'leads to a slight overlapping of flesh in the region of the shoulders', so that 'linked thus bodily together each one of us is at the same time tormentor and tormented pedant and dunce wooer and wooed speechless and afflicted with speech in the dark the mud' (153). We are not souls in search of one another, looking for someone to love, or for a reason to be, to continue to crawl through the mud, from part one to part three. Rather, 'in reality we are one and all from the unthinkable first to the no less unthinkable last glued together in a vast imbrication of flesh without breach or fissure' (153).

One can't love under these circumstances; but *How It Is* is not without love, as Leopardi's poetry and thought are not without love. It is part of Leopardi's legacy to Beckett, to find that love, and life itself as a function of that love, persists in its disavowal, not through any resistance to the logic of that disavowal but through an absolute fidelity to it. As Leopardi writes in the *Zibaldone*, the forces that sustain life are not opposed to those that eradicate it, but those forces are one and the same: 'the soul receives life (if only fleetingly) from the very forces with which it feels the perpetual death of things, and its own death' (Z261). This is the central proposition of *How It Is*, the motor that propels these creatures through the mud; and it is the force, too, that opens a distance between mouth and ear, so the sound of voice and song passes over the narrow region of the text, over the breach or fissure between first and last, here and there, speaker and hearer, that opens by virtue of the demand that it must close. Aesthetic pleasure, Leopardi writes, in a passage we quoted earlier, arises from a 'song' that is 'heard from afar or that seems far away without being so, or that is gradually fading and becoming imperceptible'; it is a song, or a voice, 'that is so distant, in appearance or in truth, that the ear and the mind all but lose it in the vastness of space' (Z1928). The desire for an encounter with naked nature in *How It Is* tends to banish that pleasure, to banish the distance which opens between people, moments and places, the distance across which sound becomes imperceptible. *How It Is* seeks that state imagined in the 'Chorus of the

Dead', in which our naked nature 'rests' in 'death'. Leopardi's dead, like Beckett's, look back on life, from some posthumous place. 'As a confused / And vaguely troubling / Memory, / So we remember / Our own lives', Leopardi writes, while Beckett's creatures are granted the odd glimmering image of life above in the light, a life 'said to have been mine', even though the 'dried-up spirit', Leopardi writes, is 'lacking strength / For hope / And for desire'. 'As, living, it shunned death, / So now our naked nature / Shuns the vital flame.' 'Ignuda natura', in Beckett and in Leopardi, shrinks from the vital differentiation that is intrinsic to living, and seeks to encase itself in unbroken flesh, the barest and most deathly life, where mouth is glued to ear. But it is the miracle of *How It Is*, to be felt in every commaless flurry of prose, that the very suffocating weight that presses these bodies together, that makes of them a 'vast imbrication of flesh', breaks them apart, opening that gap between mouth and ear in which sound might fainten, and in which the aesthetic pleasure of the text lives on.

To read *How It Is* is to open a gap, a breach in the unbroken surface of the text: 'the gaps are the holes', the narrator says, speaking to Pim, speaking as Pim; 'the holes we're talking of the holes not specified not possible no point I feel them and wait till he can' (93). From the opening line of the text, reading makes these holes happen, opening peculiar lapses, air pockets, stretches of nothingness, in which voice passes across quotation fields, into some unquoted place, some place summoned by the voice, but not contained by it. 'How it was I quote before Pim with Pim after Pim how it is three parts I say it as I hear it' (7). From this opening moment onwards, one can feel the mobility, the rhythmic movement between the eradication and the persistence of difference that is the subject of this text, and its formal and aesthetic principle. One can see and hear the distance that opens between the I that says and the I that hears, even as it is forced to close; one can hear and see it more intensely, the more intensely it is banished. The lack of punctuation – the lack of quotation marks to fence off speech, or commas to space and time it – means that reading becomes, itself, this parcelling out, this summoning of distance and difference and differentiation from their absence, their impossibility. 'I have journeyed', the narrator says, a third of the way into part one, 'found Pim lost Pim it is over I am in part three after Pim how it was how it is I say it as I hear it' (21).

I say it as I hear it, the voice says, insisting, again and again, on the closed gap between saying and hearing, mouth and ear. This text we are reading is already over, the voice says. This narrative agent you can hear is already in part three. That, he says, 'is where I have my life'. But of course, we are not in part three. We are in part one. We are on page 21, bottom paragraph. When the voice says it is in part three, it is speaking across the vast tract of this text, this region that Beckett and Leopardi map out together, across which the sound of narrative voice passes, and which is the ground, the very possibility of literary being.

This is the final discovery of *How It Is*, this summoning of an impassable distance between speaker and hearer from its eradication. This is where Beckett's tireless rehearsal of Leopardi's chiasmus takes him, and this too is the outcome of the contradiction, in both writers, between persistence and indifference, something and nothing, love and violence; between a thoroughgoing scepticism and a kind of unavoidable, unillusioned investment in literary and political possibility. Matha Nussbaum, in her moving reading of the 'genealogy of love' in Beckett's fiction, concludes that Beckett's nihilistic tendencies emerge from and result in a failure of the difference between self and other, upon which the possibility of a certain model of love relies. 'One thing that becomes clear', she writes, 'as we read these novels, is that we are hearing, in the end, but a single human voice, not the conversation of diverse human voices with diverse structures of feeling' (Nussbaum, 1990, 308). Whatever model of love Beckett leaves us with, Nussbaum suggests, it is one that is devoted to silence, solitude, solipsism; but the dialogue we have imagined here between Leopardi and Beckett suggests a different kind of loving, one that survives the most brutal equation of love with violence, and that arises from the failure of the attempt to make of two voices a single voice, of two bodies a single body. The world is mud, Beckett and Leopardi tell us; 'it's mathematical', 'it's our justice'. We are all consigned to life 'in this muck where all is identical'. But identity, for Bruno, Vico, Leopardi, Joyce, Beckett, yields duplication. It's mathematical. And whatever possibility of love, or justice, or hope these writers discover rests on this identity of the identical and the non-identical. We could have done with other loves, perhaps. But this is the one that Beckett and Leopardi allow us.

Conclusion: 'Another Heavenly Day'

The late works of our two writers create very different worlds. Most notably, perhaps, there is no more mud, no more of the primal slime from which traditionally humanity had been thought to emerge and from which, both Leopardi and Beckett believed, it had ever failed to extricate itself. The settings of their works now became, if anything, harsher, more indifferent to the needs and desires of their puny inhabitants.

Leopardi moved to Naples in 1833, and then three years later he and his friend Antonio Ranieri retired to a villa at the foot of Vesuvius, fleeing the outbreak of cholera in the city. The pair would return to Naples the next year – Leopardi would die there several months later – but it is the spectacular landscape of the volcano that would provide the forbidding setting for his two last poems, 'Broom, or The Flower of the Desert' and 'The Setting of the Moon'. Of the two, the former has drawn most critical attention, though it is thought by many that 'The Setting of the Moon' was written shortly after 'Broom' and thus has the distinction of being the very last poem Leopardi wrote. Both poems are concerned with forms of enlightenment – in 'Broom', Leopardi satirises the Catholic revivalists of Naples for making a return to the obfuscatory superstition of the Middle Ages (Leopardi, 1987, 125, lines 52–8), and the point is pressed home by the poem's epigraph from the Book of St John (3:19), an ironic choice of source with which to confute religious superstition: 'and men loved darkness rather than light'. The corrosive light of satire *and* of lyric thus provides the corrective, revealing a world grown inorganic and infertile, a world where even the hardy, 'blameless' broom must ultimately bow its vulnerable head (lines 305–6). Meanwhile the human generations come and go, their cities built, then convulsed and buried, their history forgotten as soon as it is made. Nature remains impervious, 'ever green' for so long that it seems to stand still ('sembra star', line 294). The poem's opening lines encompass a whole world – it is 'Una ruina' (line 32) – embracing the mountain slopes, the desert, the plain, the island of Capri, the ports of Naples and Mergellina (lines 256–7) and the 'hardened lava flows' where the traveller wanders confused when the moon fails to light his way and where the farmer and his family flee their land as the eruption begins. Moving always to incorporate more and more, the poem's expanding periods mime the motion of the all-consuming lava flowing from the mountain while registering, too, with great pathos, humanity's insignificant place amidst this cosmic turmoil. 'Broom' leaves us in no doubt that the cruellest enemy is nature, which 'giving birth / To mortals is our mother, / But in her malice a stepmother rather' (lines 124–5), and while Leopardi celebrates the dignified passivity of the desert flower which accepts, as humans should, its 'frail and wretched state' (line 117), the poem surrenders none of its anger or defiance and offers no ideological way in which those might be managed.

'The Setting of the Moon', which opens with a 'silvered' landscape and ocean, might seem to revive the motifs of the earlier idylls, but this moon is setting, about to plunge the world into a darkness which the poem compares to the passage from youth to maturity, to 'A half-life far more cruelly cursed /

Than dreadful death itself' (Leopardi, 1987, 122, lines 42–3). Now comes the curse of old age, 'the worst / Of all the evils', because 'Incolume il desio, la speme estinta', 'Desire, though unfulfilled, / Remains intact and is not stilled, / But hope has been extinguished in us—killed' (lines 47–8). The phrasing subtly reconfigures the line in 'To Himself' that had made such an impression on Beckett, 'Non che la speme, il desiderio è spento'. That declaration is emphatically rewritten here: desire is now 'incolume', 'intact', 'undiminished'. This is not at all that posthumous voice of 'The Chorus of the Dead', then, but one very much alive and afflicted by continuing, unsatisfied desire. And this brings us to what is perhaps the most remarkable feature of this final poem: for after the lunar lyricism of the first two stanzas and the discursive sobriety of the third we are suddenly presented with an explosion of light, of *sunlight*: 'Then afterwards the sun, / Everywhere blazing potent flames, / Will bathe you and the ethereal fields with streams / Of brightness, pure lucidity' (lines 59–62). Sunlight had figured, of course, in many of the *Canti*, but, as Citati (2016, 411) observes, not until now had Leopardi depicted the sun like this, in all its flaming potency. Marco Santagata also remarks on the sheer exuberance of this moment: 'Never before had we witnessed in Leopardi's poetry such a flood of light' (Santagata, 1999, 119, 121). The brightness recalls Leopardi's earlier evocation of noonday, a time at once seductive and dangerous when, as in 'To Spring' (1822), mortals might encounter gods. At this late stage, though, the gods are merely figments of the imagination and 'Broom' has already poked fun at fantasies about them visiting earth (Leopardi, 1987, 129, lines 191–6). This sun simply consumes such myths in its colossal 'lucidity'. It is at once an expression of the terrible energy of nature and of the force of reason by which humanity is often tempted as it strives to find its way. In that sense it is, Galimberti suggests, dogmatic like monotheism which reduces all life to the rule of one principle, whereas moonlight, illuminating the complex uncertainties of youth, allows other stars to shine as well (Galimberti, 1987, lxvi). Whatever we might say of this tremendous image, we are unlikely to exhaust its many contradictory meanings, even to decide whether it is deadly or life-affirming, because this flood of solar light seems also to define the very condition of our thinking, of that lucidity that is at once the gain and the price of our maturity. At the end of his life, Leopardi characteristically finds in the contradictions of this 'naked' vision the only way forward, but a way that, for all its commendable persistence, will carry mortals only to their graves. Meanwhile the sun will continue on its daily round, blazing forth with undiminished energy.

This summoning of energy from termination, persistence from an encounter with the inevitability of death, is Leopardi's closing contradiction, and, in its indecidability, its conflation of the deadly with the life-affirming, it establishes the parameters of Beckett's career-long examination of the simultaneous tenacity and poverty of the will. The region that we have mapped out in this Element, in which the progress westward towards the setting of the sun is combined with a struggle in the opposite direction – an exhausting crawl eastward along the deck which becomes, in *Worstward Ho*, a journey 'leastward' and 'worstward' (Beckett, 1992b, 119) – is contained within its poles.

Perhaps the moment in Beckett's oeuvre which reflects this late torrent of Leopardian sunlight most explicitly comes in his 1961 play *Happy Days*. The sun that arises from the dark at the close of 'The Setting of the Moon' and which will 'flood' ('Inonderà') with light the 'heavenly fields' ('eterei campi') recalls, more than the sun that has no alternative but to shine in *Murphy*, the blazing sun that shines at the opening of *Happy Days*, ushering in 'Another heavenly day' (Beckett, 2006, 138). The sun, Winnie says, polishing her spectacles as the day begins, 'bob[s] up out of dark', to shed its 'holy light' on the play's blasted landscape, to flood this desert space with a 'blaze of hellish light' (140) (a phrase that echoes Leopardi's 'lucidi torrenti'). The sun that shines here owes its regenerative qualities to its capacity not only to sustain life but also to eradicate it. It produces a total vision from its revelation of a form of apocalypse, an expulsion of the human from a landscape whose pristine desert clarity is an effect of its inhumanity. The brightness of the light in *Happy Days* pitilessly exposes the redundancy of a human apparatus when we have seen nature in its nakedness, in its original condition in which, as the young Krapp says in *Krapp's Last Tape*, 'the earth might be uninhabited' (221). The landscapes of Beckett's theatre, in *Act Without Words I* ('Desert. Dazzling light'; 203), in *Play*, *Happy Days*, *Endgame*, are aligned with what he finds, in the 1930s, in the painting of Cézanne, of Jack B. Yeats, of Watteau. These are works, Beckett writes, which are imbued with a 'sense of the ultimate *inorganism* of everything', a 'painting of pure inorganic juxtapositions, where nothing can be taken or given & there is no possibility for change or exchange' (Beckett, 2009, 540). The tendency towards the inorganic that we see in the later works of Leopardi and Beckett is captured in the empty desert spaces of Beckett's plays in which, as in Beckett's Cézanne, the 'landscape' is 'material of a strictly peculiar order, incommensurable with all human expressions' (222); a 'landscape with no velleities of vitalism' (222) which is 'by definition unapproachably alien', an 'unintelligible arrangement of atoms' (223).[14]

---

[14] For a reading of Beckett's relationship with Cézanne, see Nugent-Folan (2015).

Happy Days gives a theatrical representational form to the lucid torrent of light that closes Leopardi's poetic writing, and that marries total seeing with a failure of sight and of thought. And in the prose that follows, from *Imagination Dead Imagine* (1965) to *Worstward Ho* (1983) and *Stirrings Still* (1988), Beckett hones his pictures of naked life persisting in desert spaces – the naked nature that grows in Leopardi's verse from 'Chorus of the Dead' to 'Broom' and 'The Setting of the Moon'. The monotheistic light that closes 'The Setting of the Moon' finds its fullest expression in the light of those late prose texts, the light that admits no shadow, that 'appears to emanate from all sides and to permeate the entire space as though this were uniformly luminous down to its last particle of ambient air' (Beckett, 1995, 215). This is the light of *The Lost Ones*, and of *Imagination Dead Imagine*, a bare, blinding light, in which life persists in the most naked state imaginable, bodies in a ground, 'two white bodies, each in its semicircle' (182), bodies with no remaining humanity, no velleities of vitalism. The light is uniform, so there is no variation, no play in the image of bright and dim. Here, everything is 'all white in the whiteness' (182), the 'great whiteness unchanging' (185).

Beckett's later works give way to this brightness, this nakedness, in which all is revealed, and as a result the mechanised futility of the systems we live by comes out of hiding. But even as they do so, it is the discovery of Beckett's writing that the move towards such total exposure, towards what the young Beckett calls the 'total object' (Beckett, 1965, 101), produces its own forms of non-seeing, its own forms of shade, in which the failure of sight harbours something like the persistence of a striving to see. The 'total object', Beckett writes, in a richly Leopardian contradiction, is 'complete with missing parts' (101). Even the bleached, naked scenarios that recur in Beckett's late prose, the cylinders and rotundas in which narrative being beats at the rubber walls of its cell, turn out, as the narrator of *Worstward Ho* puts it, to be 'rife with shades' (1992b, 113), the shades that are uncovered by the radical lucidity of the late Beckettian light.

If there is a generative dialogue between Leopardi and Beckett, then it ends here, with the recognition that blinding, inhuman light contains within it a kind of shade that is the province of what passes, in both writers, for hope. The close of 'The Setting of the Moon' seems to banish such shades, such forms of non-being, with the move from moonlight to torrents of brilliant sun. Moonlight allows for 'far-flung shadows', which 'project a thousand lovely / insubstantial images and phantoms onto still waves and branches', where the brilliant light of the sun reveals a world without phantoms, without illusions, showing us with all its glorious brightness the single, certain truth that the world ends in the grave. But it is the discovery of Beckett's work, and of Leopardi's, as we have read them together here, that the lucidity of the sun, which shines as it has no alternative, reveals its own shade, reveals the forms of darkness, the imperceptible seams that are threaded into the visible light, and that are the engines of Beckettian and Leopardian persistence. The blazing light of Beckett's sun signals the end of a world, but it also tells us to begin, yet again. Stillness is a kind of stirring, *comment c'est* is an instruction to begin again, to *commencer*. It is another heavenly day. 'Begin, Winnie. [*Pause.*] Begin your day, Winnie' (Beckett, 2006, 138).

References

Ackerley, C. J. (2010), *Obscure Locks, Simple Keys: The Annotated 'Watt'*, Edinburgh: Edinburgh University Press.

Barnes, John C. (1989), 'La fortuna di Leopardi in Irlanda', in Franco Musara, Serge Vanvolsem and Lamberti R. Guglielmone (eds), *Leopardi e la cultura europea. Atti del convegno internazionale dell'Università di Lovanio, Lovanio 10–12 dicembre 1987*, Leuven: Leuven University Press and Bulzoni, pp. 39–45.

Beckett, Samuel (1965), *Proust and Three Dialogues with Georges Duthuit*, London: Calder.

Beckett, Samuel (1970), *More Pricks Than Kicks*, New York: Grove Press.

Beckett, Samuel (1972), 'Dante . . . Bruno . Vico . . Joyce', in *Our Exagmination Round His Factification for Incamination of Work in Progress*, London: Faber & Faber, pp. 5–13.

Beckett, Samuel (1976), *Watt*, London: Calder.

Beckett, Samuel (1992a), *Dream of Fair to Middling Women*, ed. Eoin O'Brian and Edith Fournier, Dublin: Black Cat Press.

Beckett, Samuel (1992b), *Nohow On: Company, Ill Seem Ill Said, Worstward Ho*, London: Calder.

Beckett, Samuel (1994), *Molloy, Malone Dies, The Unnamable*, London: Calder.

Beckett, Samuel (1995), *The Complete Short Prose, 1929–1989*, ed. S. E. Gontarski, New York: Grove Press.

Beckett, Samuel (1996), *How It Is*, London: Calder.

Beckett, Samuel (2006), *The Complete Dramatic Works*, London: Faber & Faber.

Beckett, Samuel (2009), *The Letters of Samuel Beckett, Vol. I: 1929–1940*, ed. Martha Fehsenfeld and Lois More Overbeck, Cambridge: Cambridge University Press.

Beckett, Samuel (2011), *The Letters of Samuel Beckett, Vol. II: 1941–1956*, ed. George Craig, Martha Fehsenfeld, Dan Gunn and Lois More Overbeck, Cambridge: Cambridge University Press.

Beckett, Samuel (2014a), *Echo's Bones*, ed. Mark Nixon, New York: Grove Press.

Beckett, Samuel (2014b), *The Letters of Samuel Beckett, Vol. III: 1957–1965*, ed. George Craig, Martha Fehsenfeld, Dan Gunn and Lois More Overbeck, Cambridge: Cambridge University Press.

References

Beckett, Samuel (2016), *The Letters of Samuel Beckett, Vol. IV: 1966–1989*, ed. George Craig, Martha Fehsenfeld, Dan Gunn and Lois More Overbeck, Cambridge: Cambridge University Press.

Benjamin, Walter [1933] (1999), 'Experience and Poverty', in *Selected Writings, Volume 2, Part 2, 1931–1934*, ed. Michael W. Jennings, Howard Eiland and Gary Smith, trans. Rodney Livingston et al., Cambridge, MA: Harvard University Press, pp. 731–6.

Benvenuti, Giuliana (1998), *Il disinganno del cuore: Giacomo Leopardi tra malinconia e stoicismo*, Rome: Bulzoni.

Ben-Zvi, Linda (1980), 'Samuel Beckett, Fritz Mauthner, and the Limits of Language', *PMLA*, 96:2, pp. 183–200.

Bickersteth, Geoffrey, ed. and trans. (1923), *The Poems of Leopardi*, Cambridge: Cambridge University Press.

Binni, Walter (1947), *La nuova poetica leopardiana*, Florence: Sansoni.

Bonnefoy, Yves (2001), *L'Enseignement et l'exemple de Leopardi*, Bordeaux: William Blake & Co. Editions.

Bonnefoy, Yves (2012), 'Snow in French and English', in *Beginning and End of the Snow, Début et Fin de la Neige*, trans. Emily Grosholz, Lewisburg, PA: Bucknell University Press, pp. ix–xvi.

Bosteels, Bruno (2011), *The Actuality of Communism*, London: Verso.

Bouchard, Norma (1999), 'Beckett: Reader of Leopardi', *Italian Culture*, 17:2, pp. 77–89.

Byron, Mark (2022), 'Intimations of Post-Mortality: The Genetic Dossier of Samuel Beckett's *Watt* and Its Romantic Residues'; unpublished lecture, Faculty of English, Oxford.

Carne-Ross, D. S. (1979), 'Leopardi: The Poet in a Time of Need', in *Instaurations: Essays In and Out of Literature Pindar to Pound*, Berkeley, CA: University of California Press, pp. 167–92.

Caselli, Daniela (1996), 'Beckett's Intertextual Modalities of Appropriation: The Case of Leopardi', *Journal of Beckett Studies*, 6:1, pp. 1–24.

Caselli, Daniela (2009), *Beckett's Dantes: Intertextuality in the Fiction and Criticism*, Manchester: Manchester University Press.

Caselli, Daniela, ed. (2010), *Beckett and nothing: Trying to understand Beckett*, Manchester: Manchester University Press.

Caselli, Daniela (2012), 'Beckett and Leopardi', in S. E. Gontarski (ed.), *The Beckett Critical Reader: Archives, Theories and Translations*, Edinburgh: Edinburgh University Press, pp. 135–51.

Cauchi-Santoro, Roberta (2016), *Beyond the Suffering of Being: Desire in Giacomo Leopardi and Samuel Beckett*, Florence: Florence University Press.

Citati, Pietro (2016), *Leopardi*, Milan: Mondadori.

Clément, Bruno (1994), 'A Rhetoric of Ill-Saying', *Journal of Beckett Studies*, 4:1, pp. 35–54.

Cohn, Ruby (2005), *A Beckett Canon*, Ann Arbor, MI: University of Michigan Press.

Cortellesa, Andrea (2006), 'E fango è il mondo: Beckett e Leopardi', in Giancarlo and Andrea Cortellesa (eds), *Tegole dal cielo; la letteratura italiana nell'opera di Beckett*, Rome: Edup, pp. 111–20.

Croce, Benedetto (1923), *La poesia e non-poesia: note sulla letteratura europea nel secolo decimonono*, Bari: Laterza.

Croce, Benedetto (1943), *Poesia antica e moderna*, Bari: Laterza.

Damiani, Rolando (1998), *All'apparir del vero: Vita di Giacomo Leopardi*, Milan: Mondadori.

De la Durantaye, Leland (2016), *Beckett's Art of Mismaking*, Cambridge, MA: Harvard University Press.

Deleuze, Gilles (1997), *Essays Critical and Clinical*, trans. Daniel W. Smith and Michael A. Greco, Minneapolis, MN: University of Minnesota Press.

Deleuze, Gilles, and Felix Guattari (1987), *A Thousand Plateaus*, trans. Brian Massumi, Minneapolis, MN: University of Minnesota Press.

De Robertis, Domenico (1986), 'Sul *Coro di morti* di Leopardi', *Rivista di letteratura italiana*, IV:2, pp. 655–79.

D'Intino, Franco (1995), *Giacomo Leopardi: Scritti e frammenti autobiografici*, Rome: Salerno Editrice.

D'Intino, Franco (2012), *Giacomo Leopardi: Volgarizzamenti in prosa 1822–1827*, Venice: Marsilio Editore.

Ebenstein, Joanna, ed. (2022), *Frederick Ruysch and His Thesaurus Anatomicus: A Morbid Guide*, Cambridge, MA: MIT Press.

Eliot, T. S. (2019), *The Letters of T. S. Eliot, Volume 8: 1936–38*, ed. Valerie Eliot and John Haffenden, London: Faber & Faber.

Epictetus (2014), *Discourses, Fragments, Handbook*, trans. Robin Hard et al., Oxford: Oxford University Press.

Esposito, Robert (2012), *Living Thought: The Origins and Actuality of Italian Philosophy*, trans. Zakiya Hanati, Stanford, CA: Stanford University Press.

Fedi, Francesca (1997), *Mausolei di sabbia: Sulla cultura figurativa di Leopardi*, Lucca: Maria Pacini Fazzi Editore.

Fortini, Franco (1946), 'La leggenda di Recanati', in Marco Forti and Sergio Pautasso (eds), *Il Politecnico: Antologia critica*, Milan: Lerici, pp. 34–8.

Foscolo, Ugo (2009), *Sepulchres*, trans. J. G. Nichols, Richmond: Oneworld Classics.

Furlani, Andre (2024), 'Leopardi in Beckett's Late Modernist Romanticism', in Michela Bariselli, Davide Crosara, Antonio Gambacorta and Mario Martino (eds), *Samuel Beckett's Italian Modernisms: Traditions, Texts, Performance*, New York: Routledge, pp. 31–53.

Fynsk, Christopher (1991), 'Foreword', in Jean-Luc Nancy, *The Inoperative Community*, ed. Peter Connor, trans. Peter Connor et al., Minneapolis, MN: University of Minnesota Press, pp. vii–xxxv.

Galimberti, Cesare (1986), *Linguaggio del vero in Leopardi*, Florence: Olschki.

Galimberti, Cesare (1987), 'Leopardi: meditazione e canto', in Giacomo Leopardi, *Poesia e Prose, Vol. 1: Poesie*, Milan: Mondadori, pp. xiii–lxxix.

Gentile, Giovanni, ed. (1918), *Operette morali, con proemio e note*, Bologna: Zanichelli.

Geulincx, Arnold (2006), *Ethics: With Samuel Beckett's Notes*, ed. Han van Ruler and Anthony Uhlmann, trans. Martin Wilson, Leiden: Brill.

Giorni, Guglielmo (1988), 'Coincidentia oppositorum, Il "Coro di morti" di Leopardi', in Ottave Besome et al. (eds), *Forme e vicende: Per Giovanni Pozzi*, Padua: Editore Antenore, pp. 475–95.

Gramsci, Antonio (1994), *Letters from Prison, Volume 2*, ed. Frank Rosengarten, trans. Raymond Rosenthal, New York: Columbia University Press.

Katz, Daniel (2003), 'Beckett's Measures: Principles of Pleasure in *Molloy* and *First Love*', *Modern Fiction Studies*, 49:2, pp. 246–60.

Keanie, Emma (2024), 'Beckett's Romantic Imagination', unpublished PhD thesis, University of Reading.

Keats, John (1982), *Complete Poems*, Cambridge, MA: Harvard University Press.

Knowlson, James (1996), *Damned to Fame: The Life of Samuel Beckett*, New York: Simon & Schuster.

Kooijmans, Luuc (2022), 'Artist of Death', in Joanna Ebenstein (ed.), *Frederick Ruysch and His* Thesaurus Anatomicus*: A Morbid Guide*, Cambridge, MA: MIT Press, pp. 13–16.

Leopardi, Giacomo (1906), *Scritti vari inediti dalle carte napoletane*, Florence: Le Monnier.

Leopardi, Giacomo (n.d. [1913?]), *Prose, con uno studio di Pietro Giordani*, Milan: Istituto Editoriale Italiano.

Leopardi, Giacomo (1936), *I Canti: seguiti dai Paralipomeni della Batracomiomachia*, ed. Ettore Fabietti, Milan: Casa per Edizioni Popolari.

Leopardi, Giacomo (1976), *The War of the Mice and the Crabs*, trans. Ernesto Caserta, Chapel Hill, NC: UNC Department of Romance Languages.

Leopardi, Giacomo (1982), *Operette Morali / Essays and Dialogues*, trans. Giovanni Cecchetti, Berkeley, CA: University of California Press.

Leopardi, Giacomo (1987), *Poesie e Prose, Vol. 1: Poesie*, ed. Mario Andrea Rigoni, Milan: Mondadori.
Leopardi, Giacomo (1988), *Poesie e Prose, Vol. 2: Prose*, ed. Rolando Damiani, Milan: Mondadori.
Leopardi, Giacomo (1998), *The Letters of Giacomo Leopardi 1817–1837*, ed. and trans. Prue Shaw, Leeds: Northern Universities Press.
Leopardi, Giacomo (2008), 'Tim Chilcott Literary Translations: Leopardi, Canti', www.tclt.org.uk, pp. 52–71.
Leopardi, Giacomo (2010), *Canti*, trans. Jonathan Galassi, New York: Farrar Straus Giroux.
Leopardi, Giacomo (2013a), *Zibaldone*, ed. Michael Caesar and Franco D'Intino, trans. Kathleen Baldwin, Richard Dixon, David Gibbons, Ann Goldstein, Gerard Slowey, Martin Thom and Pamela Williams, New York: Farrar, Straus and Giroux.
Leopardi, Giacomo (2013b), *Discourse of an Italian on Romantic Poetry*, ed. Fabio A. Camilletti, trans. Fabio A. Camilletti and Gabrielle Sims, London: Routledge.
Leopardi, Giacomo (2019), *Canti, Volume 1*, ed. Luigi Blasucci, Varese: Fondazione Pietro Bembo.
Leopardi, Giacomo (2021), *Canti, Volume 2*, ed. Luigi Blasucci, Varese: Fondazione Pietro Bembo.
Lonardi, Gilberto (1982), 'Il *Coro di morti* nel sistema poetico leopardiano', in *Leopardi e la letteratura italiana dal Duecento dal Seicento*, Atti del IV Convegno internazionale di studi leopardiano, Recanati 13–16 settembre 1978, Florence: Olschki, pp. 655–79.
Lonardi, Gilberto (1989), 'Leopardi a se stesso', *Le Forme e la Storia*, 1:2, pp. 21–36.
Luporini, Cesare (1947), *Leopardi progessivo*, Rome: Editori Rinuti.
Marcus Aurelius (2002), *Meditations: A New Translation*, trans. Gregory Hays, New York: Modern Library.
Monteverdi, Angelo (1967), *Frammenti critici leopardiani*, Naples: Edizioni Scientifiche Italiane.
Murphy, Timothy S. (2012), *Antonio Negri: Modernity and the Multitude*, Cambridge: Polity Press.
Negri, Antonio (2015), *Flower of the Desert: Giacomo Leopardi's Poetic Ontology*, trans. Timothy S. Murphy, Albany, NY: SUNY Press.
Nietzsche, Friedrich (1968), *The Will to Power*, trans. Walter Kaufmann and R. J. Hollingdale, New York: Vintage Books.
Nixon, Mark (2011), *Samuel Beckett's German Diaries, 1936–1937*, London: Continuum.

References

Nugent-Folan, Georgina (2015), 'Personal Apperception: Samuel Beckett, Gertrude Stein, and Paul Cézanne's "La Montagne Sainte-Victoire"', *Samuel Beckett Today/Aujourd'hui*, 27, pp. 87–101.

Nussbaum, Martha C. (1990), *Love's Knowledge: Essays on Philosophy and Literature*, Oxford: Oxford University Press.

Orcel, Michel (2005), 'Notes' to Orcel (trans.), *Leopardi, Chants / Canti: Traduction et présentation*, Paris: Flammarion, pp. 288–328.

Ovid (1971), *Metamorphoses, Volume 1*, trans. Frank Justus Miller, Cambridge, MA: Harvard University Press.

Petrarch (1996), *The Canzoniere or Rerum vulgarium fragmenta*, trans. Mark Musa, Bloomington, IN: Indiana University Press.

Quigley, Gabriel (2024), 'Beckett's Unwarranted Miracles: Pascal, Geulincx, Kleist', in Michael Krimper and Gabriel Quigley (eds), *Beckett Ongoing: Aesthetics, Ethics, Politics*, New York: Palgrave Macmillan, pp. 95–118.

Rabaté, Jean-Michel (2016), *Think Pig! Beckett at the Limit of the Human*, New York: Fordham University Press.

Rennie, Nicholas (2005), *Speculating on the Moment: The Poetics of Time and Recurrence in Goethe, Leopardi, and Nietzsche*, Göttingen: Wallstein Verlag.

Rota, Paolo (1996), 'Giacomo Leopardi: A se stesso', in Gian Marco Anselmi, Alfredo Cottignoli and Emilio Pasquini (eds), *Breviario dei classici italiani: guida all'interpretazione di testi esemplari*, Milan: Mondadori, pp. 194–203.

Sanguinetti, Edoardo (2000), 'Leopardi e la Rivoluzione', in *Il chierico organico: scritture e intellettuali*, Milan: Feltrinelli, pp. 113–19.

Santagata, Marco (1999), '"Il tramonto della luna", o dell'asimmetria', in *Il tramonto della luna e altri studi su Foscolo e Leopardi*, Naples: Liguori, pp. 87–121.

Singh, Ghan (1968), *Leopardi e l'Inghilterra*, Florence: Le Monnier.

Singh, Sonam (2012), 'Baudelaire without Benjamin: Contingency, History, Modernity', *Comparative Literature*, 64:4, pp. 407–28.

Spitzer, Leo (1963), 'L'Aspasia di Leopardi', *Cultura neolatina*, X–XIII, pp. 113–45.

Thomson, James (1905), *Essays, Dialogues and Thoughts of Giacomo Leopardi (Operette Morali and Pensieri)*, ed. Bertram Dobell, London: G. Routledge.

Timpanaro, Sebastiano (1979), 'The Pessimistic Materialism of Giacomo Leopardi', *New Left Review*, 1:116, pp. 29–50.

Timpanaro, Sebastiano (1985), *Antileopardiani e neomoderati nella sinistra italiana*, Pisa: ETS.

Tucker, David (2012), *Samuel Beckett and Arnold Geulincx: Tracing 'a Literary Fantasia'*, London: Bloomsbury.

Van Hulle, Dirk (2009), 'Beckett's Principle of Reversibility: Chiasmus and the "Shape of Ideas"', *Samuel Beckett Today/Aujourd'hui*, 21, pp. 179–92.

Van Hulle, Dirk and Mark Nixon (2013), *Samuel Beckett's Library*, Cambridge: Cambridge University Press.

Vecce, Carlo (2000), *Tre letture leopardiane*, Recanati: Edizioni CSNL.

Weller, Shane (2009), 'The Art of Indifference: Adorno's Manuscript Notes on *The Unnamable*', in Daniela Guardamagna and Rossanna M. Sebellin (eds), *The Tragic Comedy of Samuel Beckett; "Beckett in Rome" 17–19 April* 2008, Rome: Editori Laterza, pp. 223–37.

Williams, Pamela (2004), *An Introduction to Leopardi's Canti*, Hull: Troubadour Publications.

Zurbrugg, Nicholas (1988), *Beckett and Proust*, Totowa: Barnes & Noble.

Acknowledgements

We are grateful to friends who read and commented on the manuscript as it progressed; special thanks to Peter Middleton, Zakir Paul, Richard Sieburth, and Henry Weinfield. Our gratitude goes also to the anonymous readers for the Elements series. Thanks to Mark Nixon for reading the final manuscript with great care and attention, and to Felinda Sharmal and Lori Heaford for preparing the book for press.

About the Author

Peter Nicholls is Emeritus Henry James Professor of English and American Letters at New York University. His publications include Ezra Pound: Politics, Economics and Writing (1984), Modernisms: A Literary Guide (2nd ed. 2009), George Oppen and the Fate of Modernism (2007), and many articles and essays on literature and theory. He has co-edited a number of volumes, including The Cambridge History of Twentieth-Century English Literature (2004), Ruskin and Modernism 2001), and How Abstract Is It? Thinking Capital Now (2016). He is currently writing a book about Leopardi.

Peter Boxall is Goldsmiths' Professor of English Literature at the University of Oxford, and a Fellow of the British Academy. His books include Twenty-First-Century Fiction (2013), The Value of the Novel (2015), and The Prosthetic Imagination (2020), and his edited collections include 1001 Books (2006), and the Cambridge Companion to British Fiction: 1980–2018 (2019). He has been editor of Textual Practice since 2009. His volume of collected essays, The Possibility of Literature, came out in 2024, and he is currently at work on a book entitled Fictions of the West.

Cambridge Elements

Beckett Studies

Dirk Van Hulle
University of Oxford
Dirk Van Hulle is Professor of Bibliography and Modern Book History at the University of Oxford and director of the Centre for Manuscript Genetics at the University of Antwerp.

Mark Nixon
University of Reading
Mark Nixon is Professor of Modern Literature and Beckett Studies at the University of Reading and the Co-Director of the Beckett International Foundation.

About the Series
This series presents cutting-edge research by distinguished and emerging scholars, providing space for the most relevant debates informing Beckett studies as well as neglected aspects of his work. In times of technological development, religious radicalism, unprecedented migration, gender fluidity, environmental and social crisis, Beckett's works find increased resonance. Cambridge Elements in Beckett Studies is a key resource for readers interested in the current state of the field.

Cambridge Elements

Beckett Studies

Elements in the Series

Beckett's Intermedial Ecosystems: Closed Space Environments across the Stage, Prose and Media Works
Anna McMullan

Samuel Beckett and Cultural Nationalism
Shane Weller

Absorption and Theatricality: On Ghost Trio
Conor Carville

Carnivals of Ruin: Beckett, Ireland, and the Festival Form
Trish McTighe

Beckett and Stein
Georgina Nugent

Insufferable: Beckett, Gender and Sexuality
Daniela Caselli

Bad Godots: 'Vladimir Emerges from the Barrel' and Other Interventions
S. E. Gontarski

Beckett and Cioran
Steven Matthews

Beckett and Derrida
James Martell

Pilgrim's Gress: The Beckett Walk
Andre Furlani

Suzanne Dumesnil, Suzanne Beckett
Emilie Morin

Beckett and Leopardi
Peter Boxall and Peter Nicholls

A full series listing is available at: www.cambridge.org/EIBS

Printed by Integrated Books International,
United States of America